RECYCLED *Elegance*

*Also by Joan
and Don Bingham*

TUTTLE DICTONARY OF
ANTIQUES & COLLECTIBLES TERMS

BUYING AND SELLING
ANTIQUES & COLLECTIBLES

RECYCLED
Elegance

＋━━━＋

DECORATING
WITH
SECONDHAND
TREASURES

＋━━━＋

DON & JOAN
BINGHAM

HASTINGS HOUSE

Special Thanks

The publisher and the authors of *Recycyled Elegance* would like to give special thanks to **Golden Oldies** for giving us permission to use its photo of antique and used furniture on our front cover. **Golden Oldies**, located in a huge warehouse at 132-29 33rd Street, Flushing, New York, sells at reasonable prices, antique and replica furniture from armoires and chairs to desks, old lamps and vintage airplanes.

Hastings House
50 Washington Street
Norwalk, CT 06854

Library of Congress Cataloging-in-Publication Data is available.

ISBN 0-8038-9408-2

Distrbuted to the trade by Publishers Group West
Berkeley, CA

Printed in the United States of America

10 9 8 7 6 5 4 3 2 1

*To all the great people
we've met in
the wonderful world
of secondhand.*

ACKNOWLEDGMENTS

*F*ew books see the light of day without the cooperation of many people. We're grateful to the following folks who helped us, in large ways and small, to make this book a reality:

Our dear friends, Ottone and Dolores Riccio, for abandoning their busy schedules to take photos in their wonderful home...

Jessica Watts for the great pictures she generously provided...

Phyllis and Allan Watts who introduced us to the wonderful world of secondhand so many years ago...

Tom, Anne, Cathy, and Bill Hall, and the staff of Tom Hall's Auction Gallery in Schnecksville, Pennsylvania for welcoming us, camera and all, and for sharing their expertise...

Hy Steirman, Editor-and-chief of Hastings House for having confidence in our idea and for putting up with our nit-picking...

Cindy LaBreacht for what we think is a simply sensational book design...

Tom Tafuri for creating an inviting cover—an essential ingredient for any book...

A big thanks to all of you!

CONTENTS

INTRODUCTION

Welcome to the wonderful world of secondhand where—armed with the information in this book—you'll find tremendous bargains in furniture, accessories, dinnerware, tools, frills, and necessities—practically everything you need to furnish, decorate, and manage your home. We've been in the business of selling antiques and collectibles for many years, and we've been (and still are) amazed at the low prices merchandise brings once it's pre-owned. Through the years, we've watched as furniture from some of the finest manufacturers in the country has sold for a pittance—good, solid pieces in excellent condition. We have, in fact, furnished and accessorized our own home with secondhand treasures.

You may wonder why, if this way of buying is so great, it has been overlooked by the general public for so long? We consider this one of the great mysteries of our time, and in trying to solve it we've come up with two possible explanations. First, we've concluded that the word "secondhand" conjures up worn, inferior products in many minds. There's a stigma to buying used goods. The uninitiated wonder why anyone would do such a thing if they can afford to go to the furniture store, the department store, or the hardware store and purchase brand-new, shiny merchandise? Who wants someone else's cast offs? Second, others divide secondhand furnishings into two categories—antiques (which they know they can't afford) and junk (which they know they don't want). In truth, the average person just has no idea of what can be found in the various secondhand markets.

Take auctions, for instance. We've found so many interesting articles for our home at these sales that we'd never have been able to afford on the primary market. We're not talking Sotheby's and Christie's here but the smaller auctions, the estate auctions, the contents of the homes of real people who for any of number of reasons need or want to sell their possessions. And we don't necessarily mean antiques either—unless you want to have antiques and are willing to pay the prices they bring, and you'll certainly find them at auctions for less than you'll pay in an antiques store. (As a point of reference, you should be aware that the word "antique," as defined by the U.S. customs, refers to any article that's 100 or more years of age. But in common usage, an item that's forty or fifty years old is often called antique, and many dealers use this as their yardstick.) The merchandise on which you're going to bid will probably be of a more recent vintage. Some of what you'll find will be a wonderful quality that if it were new would sell for many times what you'll pay for it at auction.

Our purpose in writing this book is to acquaint you with the various ways of acquiring terrific furnishings and accessories for your home in the secondary markets. Even more important, we'll give you the benefit of our mistakes, because we know that forearmed with this knowledge you can avoid costly errors. We'll delve into the various furniture styles, the reproductions, the necessity for cultivating the ability to recognize quality even when it's covered with dust and to mentally remove a piece from its setting and visualize it in your home.

Obtaining the furniture, the accessories, the tools, the drapes, the lighting, the pictures, and the floor coverings is only the beginning. In this book you'll learn how to repair, to refinish, and to clean your bargains. We'll also supply basic rules of decorating, tips on working with colors and patterns, hints on buying pieces to fit your rooms, methods of assembling interesting picture groupings, instructions on placing accessories where they'll have the most eye-appeal. In short, all the knowledge you need to give your home maximum elegance with minimum expenditure.

We'll also provide information on some of the true antiques and collectibles you might like to have grace your home.

CHAPTER ONE

The Search Begins

THERE ARE MANY different types of markets where you may discover wonderful and interesting articles with which to decorate your home. All of these places are fun to shop in, and (with rare exception) all of them are infinitely less expensive than your local department or furniture store. But you need to be flexible in your decorating plan. While you can go to most any furniture store and order a sofa for $1,500 in exactly the color and style you want, the sofas you find for $100 or so in the secondary markets might cause you to reevaluate your decorating scheme. But think what you can do with the $1,400 you're saving! It will go a long way toward getting you the other furnishings you need. If you're completely redecorating or furnishing a home, you're going to be investigating most, if not all, sorts of secondary markets. You need to know where to start, and you should be familiar with what you're apt to find in each outlet. Although all types of

We found this great old oil lamp in a shop just waiting for a bargain hunter.

markets yield treasures, the ones we prefer and frequent most often are auctions.

Before you start your search through the secondhand markets, take the time to visit furniture stores, kitchen shops, and department stores in your area. Start at the classiest in each category and work your way down, comparing quality, making a list of those items you'd like to see in your home, and most of all jotting down the prices. While secondhand should be considerably less expense and usually is a bargain, there are those times when a used item will command a larger price than it can be purchased for brand new. This most often occurs at auction when two zealous bidders vie with each other. It's the direct result of a lack of knowledge— failure to do the research necessary to become familiar with true values. But it may also occur if a dealer on the secondary market is either ill-informed or a bit greedy.

Having a loose plan of what you'd like to accomplish in furnishing and decorating your home isn't essential, but it is helpful. While an eclectic decor works and can be most interesting, you don't want to end up with pieces of furniture which aren't in scale with each other or that truly don't mix well. For instance, a pair of art deco chairs would look out of place with Jacobean tables, dressy French provincial lamps wouldn't complement a primitive chest of drawers, and no matter how lovely a large statue may be it won't go in a small room. You also want your home to reflect your personality, your interests, and be conducive to your life-style. With good planning you can avoid a cluttered, hodgepodge look.

While it is best to have a plan for your home, you do need to approach the secondhand markets with an open mind and with your creative juices flowing. If you do, you're going to be surprised at the wonderful bargains that await you. Whatever type of sale you attend, take with you measurements, a pad of paper and pen or pencil, a magnet, a tape measure, and a magnifying glass.

AUCTIONS

One day a week—it's Friday in our neck of the woods—local papers list upcoming auctions. The time and place of the sale, the auctioneer's name, and a partial listing of the goods to be offered are given. If the merchandise comes from only one or two people, their names often appear in the ad—especially if the individuals are, or were, prominent in the community. We say "were" because items often come from the estates of deceased people.

Auctioneers Tom Hall and his daughter, Cathy, take turns auctioning at our personal favorite auction house in Schnecksville, Pennsylvania. The deppression cake plate was a good buy.

Looking Things Over

If the ad lists a preview time, (which may be just prior to the auction or as far in advance as several days) be there for the preview. You want the opportunity to look everything over carefully. If no preview time is given, plan to arrive about an hour before the sale is scheduled to begin. You'll probably find the doors are open.

It's not easy to assess merchandise until you actually see it. The newspaper ad will contain a partial listing of what to expect. But condition is rarely mentioned, and if it is, the auctioneer is going to describe what he has to offer in the most glowing of terms. Why? He or she wants to lure as many people as possible to the sale.

Before you even look around, grab yourself, and whomever you're with, front seats. You want to get a good look at what you're bidding on, even though you should already have examined it. And having a front seat also gives you the opportunity to hear the comments of the auction staff, who are usually quite knowledgeable. If the auction is held at an estate or any outdoor place, you'd be wise to stick a folding chair or two into your car or van.

During the preview, take a good look at everything in which you have the slightest interest. Don't just look at the upholstery on a sofa or chair. Sit in it. Look under the cushions. Turn it upside down if you can. Get a look at the springs. See if there is any label that reveals who made the piece. While it's wonderful to find an overstuffed chair or sofa with flawless upholstery, it's far more important to find furniture that's structurally sound. You can always slipcover or reupholster if you get the piece at the right price and still save bundles of money.

The Slipcover Option

If you come across the perfect chair or sofa in a worn fabric, a design that won't work for you, or a color you hate, slipcovers could be the answer. But before you take the plunge and purchase the furniture, evaluate its slipcover potential. Simple, square furniture is much easier to slipcover than pieces with lots of curves and pillows; and if a sofa or chair has decorative wood on the back or arms, it usually is a better candidate for reupholstering, as are pieces with concave backs.

If the piece is simple, you have three slipcover options:

☛ You can purchase ready made covers. Some fit surprisingly well, and the cost is relatively modest. Relative to what? you may ask. Relative to what you'll pay for option number two.

☛ Custom made slipcovers run quite high. In fact, in some instances you could purchase a new sofa or chair for what you'll pay for custom slip covers. Of course, the larger the furniture and the more involved the lines, the more it's going to cost to have slipcovers made. Lots of pillows and lots of curves not only take lots of material and lots of time but cost lots of money because the cutting and sewing is more difficult.

☛ The third option is to make your own slipcovers. It's not as daunting as it sounds if you have any talents in the sewing area. But it is too detailed to include in this book, especially since there are so many fine books in the stores and libraries covering this subject. The Singer Sewing Reference Library includes an excellent book, *Sewing Projects for the Home*, which includes easy to follow directions for slipcovering.

Other Considerations

Make sure that the legs on tables and chairs are sturdy; that the springs aren't falling out of the bottoms of the overstuffed pieces. Take a good look at frames for nicks and scratches. And, of course, take measurements. If you find a sofa or chair that's the proper size and you like the lines, sit in it before you decide if and how much you're willing to bid on it. Uncomfortable furniture is not a bargain at any price, and comfort is a subjective thing. Everyone in the family should have at least one chair in which to relax.

There are some auction houses where you'll not be permitted to examine all of the merchandise. If you're interested in a piece, one of the employees will allow you to handle that particular item. Obviously with this method you're not going to be able to go over everything that's being offered at the auction. We don't attend auctions where this practice is used.

The "try-it-out-for-size-and-comfort" rule also applies to dining room and kitchen tables and chairs. Friends of ours found a lovely cherry dining room table which was being offered at auction with six chairs upholstered in a pristine, creamy colored damask. There wasn't a scratch or blemish on the entire set. Our friends had been scouting the stores, pricing dining room furniture and knew that a set of this quality would retail for about $4,500. The bidding was brisk, but our friends offered the top bid of $1,200. It took two trips in their van to get the furniture home, and it wasn't until then that they sat in the chairs. Much to their displeasure, they found that the chair seats were a bit too high—just enough to make crossing their legs an impossibility. They concluded that the chairs and table had not been made to go together. While the set was still a bargain, and looks lovely in their dining room, had they tried the chairs before they owned them, they probably would have waited for a more comfortable arrangement.

If you're going to be purchasing linens, open them up and take a good look. Some stains can be removed, others are there to stay. If curtains or drapes are stained, note where the problem occurs. If you're going to be cutting the material to a smaller size, perhaps it will be possible to cut it so that the damaged part can be eliminated.

Write down any item in which you're interested in your notepad. How much do you think you'd be willing to pay to own it? Will both the size and design fit into your home? Put a magnet on any brass items that strike your fancy. If the lamp, statue, or figurine takes a magnet, then it's not solid brass and in most cases shouldn't sell for as much as a solid brass item would. The magnifying glass is so that you'll be able to read any backstamp that might be on a dinnerware set, a vase, or a candy dish. It will also help you discern whether or not a painting is signed. Some artists are modest with their signatures.

Notice that we said examine anything in which you have even the *slightest* interest. That's because the articles you really love may sell for much more money than you feel you can spend, while a piece that could be attractive if it weren't for a chip, a broken leg, or a large scratch may go for next to nothing. If it's the right size, and you can fix it—go for it. Many pieces of furniture are well worth the price of refinishing. You may get a table for as little as $10, spend $40 having it refinished, and end up with a lovely, solid wood table of a quality you couldn't approximate in a furniture store for less than $250. That's making good use of your decorating money.

While you're busy inspecting merchandise, you may hear someone bad-mouthing a piece in which you've shown interest. The criticism may be legitimate or the critic may be talking down a piece in which he or she is interested, hoping to cut down on the competition. There's one instance of this that we recall vividly. One spring many years ago when we were new to the auction scene, we attended a high-class estate auction. There was a beautiful Oriental rug that we'd inspected and decided was just right for our dining room. As we turned to look at something else, a woman came along, looked at the back of the rug and said in a loud voice to her friend, "There are worm eggs in this rug. It will fall apart in no time." Wow!

Were we ever glad we'd heard her and been saved from investing in a bad rug! We felt sorry for the man who won the bid on it even though it went low. Were we ever surprised when we saw the woman who'd criticized the rug and her friend carrying the carpet out of the auction. Evidently, she'd had the man bid for her so that all those who'd heard her criticism of the rug wouldn't catch on.

We no longer listen to bad-mouthing. But we do inspect carefully on our own.

The Many Faces of Auctions

There are all different types of auctions—some are chock full of just what you're looking for to furnish your home, and others feature junk, used car parts, guns, coins, stamps. There are auctions for which an auctioneer has collected merchandise from many sources. He or she may even have purchased new merchandise wholesale and have it sprinkled in with the other items. Auctions with this type of merchandise are usually held at a hall that's either owned or rented by the auctioneer.

There are estate sales. At these the merchandise usually comes from one household, although at times several estates are combined. Some auctions are held as fund raisers by institutions such as schools, hospitals, churches, or museums. At these you'll either find items that have been donated by people interested in furthering the goals of the institution or, in some cases, the institution has been willed an entire household. Institutional auctions are generally held at the institution in question, although they're occasionally conducted at an auction hall. And there are Sheriff's auctions, at which abandoned property (such as what might be left if a tenant is evicted or when someone has put items in storage and neglected to pay the rent for a protracted period of time), or property on execution (items that have been turned over to a sheriff when an otherwise indigent person has lost a law suit) are offered. There are General Services Administration Sales, which we discuss further on in this chapter.

You can get a pretty good idea of what type of merchandise is being offered by reading the ad. We've found that estate auctions are a great place to start if your goal is to furnish a home. Many estate auctions are held right at the home. Others are held at an auction house or other facility to which the merchandise has been moved.

Don't let the word "estate" fool you. It doesn't necessarily mean a mansion—although it might. The auction usually is conducted at the request of heirs who have inherited the property and its contents, senior citizens who are moving into smaller quarters, or people who are moving far enough away that they deem it financially unwise to have their possessions shipped. Both the home and it's contents may be quite modest, middle class, or elegant and impressive. These sales often yield good clean merchandise at give-away prices.

There are special perks to buying at estate auctions which are held at the "estate:" First, the furniture, pictures, rugs, and other items are being sold in the home in which they've been used. They haven't been trucked into a warehouse or auction house. Moving household goods always subjects them to dirt and damage.
Second, you have the opportunity to see the type of home the merchandise comes from. The only time this can be super important is with overstuffed pieces of furniture that might harbor bugs. Nothing takes the thrill out of acquiring a new chair quicker than finding that buffalo bugs or cockroaches are fanning out from it as they explore their new home. If you're unlucky enough to find insects in curtains, drapes, towels, tablecloths, or the like you can wash them in hot water. But it's hard to dunk a Morris chair!

Third, at estate auctions held at the home, you'll find an assortment of items that aren't usually offered at auction houses—certainly not at the better auction houses. For instance, if the auctioneer truly has full reign to sell the entire contents of the home, then whatever is in the kitchen cabinets and drawers, or on the countertops will be sold—so will the towels and sheets from the linen closets. It's odd, but we've never been to an auction held at a home where unused towels and sheets weren't put up for bid. And we've also never been to an auction held at a home where these items and all of the kitchen equipment haven't sold for a very small fraction of their real worth.

The down side is that sometimes relatives scoop off the cream of the estate for themselves and leave what nobody in the family wants for the auctioneer. The poshest of homes may offer only old, tired furniture and an uninteresting assortment of smaller items while a not-so-glitzy place holds better-cared-for stuff. A few auctioneers salt estate sales with merchandise from other sources.

Be Prepared

Before you leave for the auction, measure the spaces into which you're going to put a sofa, a chair, a dining set, and any other furniture. Carry with you a list of these measurements along with the measurements of all the windows for which you need curtains, drapes, or shades. You have some latitude in this area, for while you can't use a window treatment that's too small, you can buy drapes or curtains that are larger than you need and cut them back. Few people attend auctions in search of drapes or curtains so you're likely to find wonderful examples, often in rich materials that will give your home an elegant look, for a pittance. If curtains or drapes aren't on your "needs" list, you might still want to consider bidding on them just for the material to use for making pillows, table or dresser scarves, or curtain tie backs. Your imagination is one thing you don't want to leave behind when you go to an auction.

Speaking of taking things home, you should go to an auction, or any sale for that matter, with the means of taking whatever you purchase with you when you leave. If you can't do that, speak to a member of the auction house staff before the auction begins to find out if you can leave large items and if so for how long. If an auction is held at a firehouse or some other rented facility, chances are that all of the goods must be removed from the premises directly after the auction. If the auction is in an auction house or estate, you may be able to leave large pieces there for a day or two. But remember that from the time the auctioneer says yours is the winning bid, the piece of merchandise is yours and it is your responsibility. (Unless, as sometimes happens, the auction house holds the merchandise until it is paid for—at which time it becomes your responsibility). So if you leave a sofa, and someone else absconds with it, it's your loss. Most auction houses try very hard to see that this type of thing doesn't happen, but with all their efforts occasionally something does seem to disappear.

You also need bags or boxes in which to carry any small items you purchase and wrappers to protect precious breakables. We prefer the boxes in which fruit (usually bananas) is delivered to stores. They're a nice size, and they have cut-out handles which make them easy to carry. There are several choices for wrapping. You can use newspaper, admittedly the cheapest alternative, but the print will quickly blacken your hands as well as dirty whatever is wrapped in it. You can purchase plain white paper at any moving supply house. This is the same as newspaper sans the ink. Or you can buy chair or bed pads, which are soft and can be used over and over. You'll find these near the diapers in your grocery store. We much prefer them.

Catalogs

Many auction houses, especially when they're auctioning off good quality merchandise, provide a catalog for their customers. Some of these catalogs are free, but most of them are sold for a few dollars. We have always found them well worth the price. The physical layout of these catalogs ranges from a photocopied, typed list of the merchandise all the way to a full-color presentation. But they all list the items to be offered, usually with a description. Some of them also provide what is called "a pre-auction estimate," which is the approximate price the auctioneer expects the lot or item in question to bring. Often these estimates are right on, but at other times an item will go for far less or far more than the auctioneer anticipated. One of the most valuable aspects of these catalogs is that the items are listed by lot number in the order in which they'll be offered. This allows you to roam around, go to the snack bar, or even leave the auction hall if there's nothing you're interested in coming up soon. Without a catalog, you have to stick around or that vase, picture, or table on which you've got your heart set may be sold while you're elsewhere.

Bidding and Other Bits of Business

At almost all auctions you need a bidder's number to participate in the event. Any of the auction staff can show you where to register for one. You'll be assigned a number and given a placard, fan, or piece of paper with that number on it. When you want to bid on an item, just hold the number up so the auctioneer can see it. If you're the high bidder, the amount you're paying will be listed under your bidder's number; at the end of the auction when you check out, you'll pay the total amount recorded against your number. Be sure you keep your own record and that the amount you have tallies with the amount the auction house is charging you. People who run auction houses, like all of us, do make honest mistakes from time to time—the most common is charging an item to the wrong bidder number.

In states where there is sales tax, you'll be charged that amount on top of your purchase price. Although in some states the sales tax is waived at an estate sale. At an increasing number of auctions, you'll also have to pay a buyer's premium—usually 10 percent, so keep that in mind as you bid. (A buyer's premium is a fee charged the buyer by the auctioneer. This fee allows the auctioneer to take a smaller percent of the selling price from the owner of the merchandise that's being offered at the sale. Auction houses compete with each other to obtain goods to sell, and an auction house that takes a low percentage of the profits is enticing to anyone who wants their possessions sold at auction.)

If there is a buyer's premium, that fact should be clearly posted or at least mentioned in the ad. At most auction houses you can pay with cash, a personal check (usually it must be issued on a bank in the state where the auction takes place), a cashier's check, or a major credit card (there may be an additional charge and/or a minimum for this convenience). If you purchase a large item and are not able to take it with you on the day of the auction, some auctioneers will allow you to leave a deposit of 25 percent and pay the balance when you pick up the item in question. When paying with anything but cash, you'll need a valid form of identification, such as a driver's license.

When it comes to bidding, each auctioneer seems to have an individual style and rhythm. Some start with two bidders and keep going until one of them quits, then continue with the high bidder of the original two plus a new bidder. The bidding continues in this way until all bids are exhausted, at which point the lot goes to the high bidder. Other auctioneers take bids in sequence, going from the opening bid to the second bidder, to the third bidder and when there are no more new bidders, back to the original, until there is only one bidder left. Some auctioneers are more difficult to understand than others. We much prefer the ones who call out bids clearly. Some auctioneers chant their bids in such a manner that it's often impossible to tell whether they're asking for say $50 or $500.

When you're in doubt, it's best to abstain from bidding. No matter how much you think you want the merchandise, there will be other opportunities at other auctions. Many auctioneers, even good ones, go so fast that the audience doesn't have time to think about their bids. This is one of the reasons you need to have a top figure that you're willing to pay for an item firmly fixed in your mind when you start bidding. But if you do want time to think, drop out of the bidding. You can usually get back in at the end when auctioneers generally pause for a few seconds to make sure there are no more bids.

Auction fever is contagious. When you want an item, it's hard to curb your enthusiasm, but try to do so. Your excitement can spill over onto others in the audience, making that arm chair, sofa, or end table that's just right for your home seem much more enticing to another bidder. Another big mistake you want to avoid is bidding on someone else's knowledge. It works like this: Someone in the audience seems keen on say a vase that you sort of like. After you've reached your determined high bid on the item, the other party tops it without hesitation. You then decide that the vase must be worth far more than you'd thought and you keep bidding. Several bids later, you end up with the vase. You got it on what you perceived to be someone else's knowledge, when in fact there may have been several reasons why the other bidder wanted that particular vase: He or she may be a friend or family member of the original owner of the vase and want it for sentimental value. The vase may simply strongly appeal to the other bidder. The other bidder may own a mate to the vase. Or, ironically, the other bidder may have been bidding on *your* knowledge. You may know that the party bidding against you is a dealer. But always keep in mind that dealers don't know everything. In fact, some know very little!

One caveat for the auction goer: You're buying all merchandise "where it is and as it is." That means that from the moment you've won the bid the merchandise is your responsibility. You must see that it's in a safe place, and you must take care of transporting it. "As it is," is a reminder that you bear the burden of inspecting anything on which you wish to bid. If a piece is damaged when you get it, you still must accept it and pay for it—with a couple of exceptions. Some of the better auctioneers will allow members of the audience to return glass or china if they find a crack or chip that appears to be new. That's because you might look at that piece an hour before the auction begins and find it in perfect condition, then someone else may handle it and do damage. But in almost all cases, you need to return the item to a member of the auction house within five minutes of having purchased it. The other circumstance in which an auctioneer will take back an article that's just been sold is if the auctioneer has presented it as being in perfect condition and the bidder finds a flaw that's been overlooked. Imperfections formed in the molding or making of glass or china aren't considered damage. They're often referred to as something that "happened in the making."

Many, if not most, of the people who frequent auctions are dealers. They should not give you much competition because they need to purchase merchandise at a price that will allow them room to mark up for resale. You don't. You have the luxury of being able to outbid them. You will, however, see items go at what will seem to be outrageously inflated bids. If you're not familiar with antiques and collectibles, and there's no reason you should be, you're going to be mystified to see several dealers vying for a worn-out teddy bear, a piece of blue depression glass, or a feather Christmas tree. They may look like junk to you, and you may wonder if you can possible purchase anything at an auction where the prices are so high. Don't worry, these things are collectibles. You may want to use collectibles in your home, but only select those you like and can get at a good price. Chances are that the dealers don't want the lamps, chairs, rugs, etc. you're hoping to take home. They may, however, want the period pieces—the Victorian parlor set, the Hepplewhite table, or the Windsor desk (even if it's only a Windsor-style desk).

Box Lots

No assessment of auctions would be complete without a few words about box lots—those offerings with which auction goers have a love-hate relationship. Box lots are comprised of assortments of objects that the people setting up an auction don't deem important enough to be auctioned off individually—mismatched dishware, brick-a-brack, an assortment of picture frames, for example. Sometimes the boxes are carefully assembled and contain related items, but more often they've been put together in a hurry. Many broken items find their way into box lots, but usually there is at least one good piece per box, and sometimes you'll find a real treasure. Some of the broken pieces may serve you well. While dealers shun most broken items, you don't have to. The vase that has a hunk out of one side of the rim may look perfect on your desk if you turn the hurt side to the wall. But don't get carried away with the number of items in a box lot. Bid on each box lot as if it only contained the item or items in which you're interested. The remainder may be of no use to you and, in fact, if you buy enough box lots, you will probably throw away those items which are truly trash.

GSA Auctions

The Federal Supply Service, a branch of the federal government, has a department known as the General Services Administration or GSA. It is the job of the GSA, which has ten offices around the country, to dispose of surplus items. They most commonly do this by the auction method. Much of the merchandise they handle will not be of interest to you. Still, there may be a few good buys of just what you're looking for, making it worth pursuing this avenue of obtaining merchandise.

There are several types of GSA auctions: The *open bid* auction functions exactly like a regular auction. You go to the site where the auction is being held, get a bidder's number, and bid in competition with others until there's only one bidder left. The *spot sale* is also a sale you attend as you would a regular auction, but at which you're allowed to give only one written bid. When the bids are collected, the highest bidder gets the item on the block. The last type of GSA auction in which you might have an interest is a *sealed* bid auction. Bidders don't attend this type of sale but send their bids on a specific form to the GSA who accept the highest bid.

To find the GSA office nearest you, contact your library and ask for the address of the Personal Property Division of the GSA. Then write to the GSA at the address they supply and request to be put on their mailing list. Be aware that in sales of this type you must pick up any merchandise that your bid takes and accept it in "as is" condition.

TAG SALES

These sales usually give you another opportunity to buy merchandise from the home in which it has been used. But the sale is conducted differently from an auction. As a rule, interested people line up outside the house or apartment an hour or so before the sale is scheduled to begin. At the appointed hour, a small number of people will be allowed into the premises. As one person leaves, another will be invited in. What you'll find inside is merchandise bearing price tags. The prices have been established by salespeople who work for companies that specialize in running tag sales. There's little room for bartering at these sales. But there are often good solid bargains. These are not the kind of buys you'll find at auctions, where something may slip by for far less than it's worth, but still a deep reduction from what you'd pay for the same item if it were new.

The merchandise at tag sales is usually of a good quality. Few companies will waste their time and effort with junk. At most of these sales you can make arrangements to come back and pick up large items. You'll also see furnishings arranged as the people who owned them had them. Generally, living room items are still in the living room, bedroom things in the bedrooms, etc. This may give you some ideas on decorating with any of the furnishings you end up buying.

As we said, there is little room for bargaining at these sales, but if you see something you want and the price is more than you're willing to pay, make an offer. If it's the beginning of the sale, you'll probably be turned down. Ask if they'll reconsider your offer if the merchandise in question doesn't sell during the sale. Leave your phone number and ask for a number where one of the sales staff can be reached. This is a real long shot, but long shots do pay off sometimes. And more than one person has ended up with what they wanted by being patient at a tag sale.

YARD SALES AND GARAGE SALES

These sales are usually generated by the need of the sellers to get rid of items that have been gathering dust in attics, basements, or just around their homes for a period of time. They're most often held at the home of the seller, although sometimes several families will bring their merchandise to one home. Frequently yard sales are held by an entire neighborhood. The customers roam from home to home. Of course, you can't be at all the houses at once. We've found that people start with the first homes they come to from whatever direction they're approaching the sale. We get to these sales early and start in the middle, working our way toward the edges of the neighborhood. This way we're the first customers at several sales.

Selecting Sales

Yard and garage sales are listed in the classified section of most newspapers. Most of the listings have a brief list of some of the merchandise that's available or at least the type of merchandise. There are endless sales that feature children's clothing, for example. While they often have other items as well, few of them will

For the lover of the unusual, the secondary markets offer treasures such as this wonderful old advertising sign.

have anything in which you'll be interested. The paper will also list the address of the sale and the time it will begin. You won't be able to hit all of the sales so you need a plan of action. First, eliminate the listings which don't sound as if they'll have what you're looking for. Then try to home in on those that do have what you want—furniture, household goods, dishes, etc. Some listings are specific—some quite vague. You'll notice that the beginning time will fluctuate anywhere from 7 in the morning to noon, although most sales begin at either 8 or 9.

Obviously you can't be in more than one place at a time. Select the sale that sounds the best to you and build around it. Say, it's at 7 and it's on Main Street. Now look for another one that starts at 7 and is in the same neighborhood or at least close by. You're going to be at the one on Main Street early, and then you can zip over to that second, not as enticing, sale. Now, find the best sale at 8 and an alternate one, using the same rational and so on for 9 and 10. The sales at 7 needn't be in the same neighborhood as the ones at 8 and so forth, just as long as they're not so far afield that you can't reach the first choice in each time slot well ahead of time.

Choosing the sales is a hit-or-miss proposition. We've found that the sales that sound the least promising are sometimes filled with wonderful items and those that tout "antiques, collectibles, household goods, something for everyone," may turn out to be slim pickings. It's a little like playing the lottery, only your chances are way better.

For the most part, people who have garage or yard sales consider their merchandise "junk." The purpose of holding a sale is to get rid of things that are no longer used and pick up a few dollars in the process. And on a bright, sunny day it's fun to sit outside conversing with the people who wander through looking for a treasure or a bargain. On the other hand, there are those few people who think anything that belonged to Mom or Aunt Mable has to be very old and thus very valuable.

The Treasure Hunt

The neat thing is that there are treasures to be had. The average person probably remembers what he paid for the juicer he gave his wife for Christmas, that she hasn't even taken out of the box; the decorative pillows which never quite matched the sofa and were relegated to a closet shelf; or the cat bed that Fluffy spurned. But if the item for sale is a vase, a mirror, a lamp, or a dish that was inherited or was a gift from a well-intentioned friend or relative, chances are the seller has no idea of the value and will let it go cheap. The trouble is you, as a novice, may not spot these hidden bargains. One way to keep on your tocs is to peruse a general price guide for antiques and collectibles, such as Schroeder's Antiques Price Guide—the listing we consider the most useful. It is published annually. All you need do is familiarize yourself with names such as Noritake, Limoges, and Roseville. Then when you see an item backstamped with one of these names you can take advantage of the seller's ignorance.

Garage sales are popular fund raisers for associations, churches, schools—in short, any organization that needs to raise money for projects. For the most part, we find these sales disappointing and have decided the problem lies in the fact that the merchandise is donated. And while the members of an organization might want to support it, they usually don't donate much that's of value. If a good piece does surface, someone in the group generally scoops it up before the sale actually begins.

There are what are referred to as "professional garage salers"—people who actively seek merchandise to sell at their garage sales. They usually hold these sales on a fairly regular basis. You can still find bargains. But you're apt to find fewer under $5 items than you will at a bona fide "I'm-cleaning-out-the-closets-and-cabinets" sale.

Antiques and collectibles dealers prowl yard and garage sales, arriving as much as an hour before the sale begins, knowing that the seller is probably pretty naive about the value of what's in the sale. But you aren't really competing with the dealers. They're looking for antiques, which are rare indeed at garage sales, and collectibles, which are often found for pennies at garage sales and which the knowledgeable dealer may turn around and sell for many dollars. You're looking for items you need to outfit your home—items that hold little interest for the average dealer.

You'll find different types of merchandise in different types of selling situations. The yard and garage sale is fertile ground for such things as dishes, glasses, towels, draperies, artifacts, a plethora of baby and children's clothes, and a host of other items—including junk, junk, junk. It's a matter of sifting through and finding the roses among the thorns. A set of dishes may be missing a cup, a plate, or a saucer and still be worth considering. At the same sale, glasses may be up for grabs because they were purchased to go with those dishes and don't match the new replacement dishes the seller has bought. All they're doing is taking up valuable cabinet space. They'll sell cheap.

We think the very best type of garage sale for anyone trying to furnish a home is the "moving sale." At a true moving sale you're liable to find furniture in good condition that's being sold because it isn't going to fit into the seller's new abode. Draperies or curtains in just the colors you're looking for may be waiting for you. It's at the moving sale that you'll find your best buys. These people have to sell the items or pay to have them moved. They can't pack the leftovers away for another day and another sale. Don't be shy about making an offer far below the asking price. The seller can always say, "no," and you can always raise your offer. You can also leave an offer and your phone number should the seller be left with what you're interested in at the end of the sale. It's wise to let him or her know, however, that you're going to continue looking and you'll only be interested if you haven't found something else. This sometimes results in an immediate price reduction. We find that moving sales are well attended by people who aren't dealers so for this particular type of sale, arrive well before the appointed hour unless the ad reads "no early birds."

If you're looking for furniture, always ask the hosts at a garage sale if they have any for sale. Quite often people don't put out furniture, either figuring it isn't a garage sale item or because they don't want to lug it out of the house and then back in if it doesn't sell. They may put up a sign someplace that announces that there is furniture for sale or they may only answer inquires. At any rate, there's nothing to be lost by asking.

Become a Yankee Trader

Bargaining is an integral part of garage sales. Few people expect to actually get the price they put on an item. We always ask for the best price for any merchandise that's marked over five dollars. If we're interested in several articles at one sale, we gather them together and ask how much of a discount the seller would be willing to give if we purchased them all. Some of these might be marked less than five dollars, but we feel it's fair to expect a discount even on inexpensive items if we purchase in volume. Many sellers don't go to the bother of marking prices on their merchandise but will call out a price if you express interest. While we won't do business with a dealer at a shop or flea market who doesn't mark his items, we find it an excusable oversight at a garage sale. These are, after all, not professional merchandisers. They're merely people out to make a few dollars on items they're discarding.

People who run garage sales aren't looking for repeat business, so they're not apt to refund money if you find that a piece is damaged after you've paid for it. Look everything over carefully before you put down your money. There may be defects that won't affect your desire to buy an item. If this is the case, politely point out the flaw; the seller may reduce the price accordingly. Recently we found a silver plate tea service in its original box with all the pieces, including the teapot, creamer, sugar, and a tray—still factory wrapped. It was definitely an unwanted gift—the card was still with the set. We were delighted. For only eight dollars, instead of the ten that was asked, we purchased this find. When we got it home, however, we found that one of the feet on the teapot had broken off. We hadn't looked over the set carefully enough—our loss! We discussed repairing the leg, but we concluded that soldering would show, and the set wasn't valuable enough to warrant a professional mending.

It's at garage sales that you'll find practical items such as glasses, dishes, drapes, and sheets, as well as accessories. This is the avenue many people take to dispose of unwanted gifts from relatives and friends. Newlyweds commonly put out wedding gifts that don't fit into their decorating schemes. Small appliances surface at garage sales, too. We highly recommend that you not only ask if an appliance works but that you try it out before you purchase it. Most people are accommodating when it comes to this. If someone is loathe to let you plug in a toaster, vacuum cleaner, or coffee maker, chances are there's something wrong with it. Pass it by, no matter how good the price may seem.

In the case of large appliances, ask if the seller will give you any guarantee. He probably won't, but the appliance may still be worth taking a chance on if the price is low enough. If you're lucky, you may be able to talk the seller into guaranteeing the item for a week or two. That's enough time to try the appliance. Be sure to get any instruction booklets that go with an appliance. There's nothing worse than getting your "bargain" home and realizing you don't have any idea how to use it.

Tools and gardening equipment are frequent garage sale finds and generally are marked very low. The man who just bought a rider mower may be selling an electric or gas mower that's in beautiful shape just because he doesn't want to store it any longer.

SECONDHAND SHOPS

Strictly Speaking, the toniest antique store is still just a second-hand shop, but this isn't the type of store where you'll find inexpensive elegance. Every city and most towns have stores exclusively dedicated to selling used merchandise. There are profit and nonprofit secondhand shops. Strange as it may seem, you're more apt to find what you want for your home at a good price at a shop that's run by someone looking to make a profit. These people purchase their merchandise and, because they intend to turn it around as quickly as possible, they're selective about what they choose. The nonprofit shops, such as Good Will or the Salvation Army, rely heavily on donated goods, and as we stated earlier, people don't usually donate high-quality merchandise. However, it may be worth your while to take a quick look in a nonprofit shop. Occasionally something does turn up. We once found a lovely Oriental vase at a thrift shop. Another visit to this type of store yielded a fine, old figural lamp. It was in excellent condition after we cleaned off the layers of grime.

A Good Nose and a Poker Face

Many secondhand shops are a maze of clutter. Don't be put off by this. Systematically work your way through the store, examining everything and reacting to nothing. Your enthusiasm could cost you money when it comes time to bargain with the proprietor. We avoid purchasing upholstered pieces in these shops unless we know the dealer and can rely on his word if he tells us that a piece came from a clean home. But we've found some delightful accessories and several pieces of wood furniture over the years. Use your nose in determining the condition of merchandise unless it's porcelain or some other material that can be easily washed. A lovely looking end table may have absorbed enough moisture from being inadequately stored to give it an offensive, musty smell. This is very difficult to overcome.

Solid comfort dressed in velvet—this modern chair brought only $15 at an auction.

The Bottom Line

If you make a selection in a secondhand store, feel free to bargain. The sales people will expect this. (Although they'll be happier if you're willing to pay full price. Have a fixed amount in your mind of what the item is worth to you. If you're not sure whether the item is going to work in your home, ask if you might try it with a money-back guarantee—not a merchandise exchange. Some store owners are very obliging about this and allow customers to return things if they do so within a day or two. This is especially true if you're a repeat customer and have established some sort of rapport with the shopkeeper.

Don't expect the prices at secondhand stores to be as low as they are at garage sales or auctions. After all the shop owner had to spend time finding it, spend money purchasing it, and probably expend energy cleaning it; and he or she is in business to make a profit, if not a living. But if you find what you want in one of these shops—buy it. You could wait a long time before that particular article appears at an auction or garage sale.

FLEA MARKETS

Indoor and outdoor, seasonal and year-round, flea markets have become thriving businesses where people from all walks of life deal in new and used merchandise of all descriptions. Most of these markets are poor sources of furniture, but offer just about anything else you're looking for to set up housekeeping. For the most part, these dealers aren't as knowledgeable as those whom you'll encounter in secondhand stores or at tag sales so your chances for a real bargain are significantly increased.

Haggling over prices is standard practice. If it's an outdoor market, you may get your best buys at the end of the day when weary vendors want to unload merchandise so they won't have to pack it and transport it home.

The rules for flea markets are much the same as those for garage sales—go early for the best choices and late for the best bargains.

COOPS

Many coops are large, and because of this there's a lot of merchandise to consider. The number of these markets has increased many fold over the last few years. The concept is that many individual dealers rent space under one roof. In some of these establishments, the dealers man their own space at all times. But at most coops a few of the dealers are on duty at any given time. Every dealer takes a turn at working or hires someone else to work in his or her place. The dealers who are working are responsible for selling merchandise for the dealers who aren't there.

Some of these establishments are quite strict about what can be sold. Others have few rules. If the rules are lax enough, the coop takes on the ambiance of a flea market.

It's difficult to bargain in most coops unless the dealer who owns the merchandise in which you're interested happens to be on duty. Most dealers aren't authorized to reduce the price of another dealer's things. But, if you ask, you may find that you'll be given the 10 percent discount that's a fairly standard courtesy dealers give one another. If the item in which you're interested is a big-ticket one, one of the dealers on duty may be willing to contact the owner of that item and ask about a better price for you.

THE CLASSIFIEDS

The last, and we think the least, of the sources for secondhand merchandise is to be found in the classified section of newspapers. It's seldom that we've found anything in these columns that has interested us. And we've visited some pretty disreputable places following up on ads. But if you see a compelling listing under Articles for Sale, Bargain Box, or a similar heading, by all means

call. You may find just what you're looking for. The world of secondhand is full of surprises.

   With the descriptions and tips from this chapter, you should
be ready to start your search of the secondhand markets. Whether
you're looking for a few items or furnishings for an entire home,
we hope you have as much fun finding bargains and unusual treasures as we've had over the years.

CHAPTER TWO

Creating the Background

THERE ARE MAJOR choices to be made in setting the scene that will provide a background for your furniture and accessories. The skill with which you approach this task will be a paramount part of your success or failure. You need the right floor coverings and wall decorations. You need adequate lighting and the right window treatments. The information in this chapter will enable you to set the mood you're looking for in your home.

FLOOR COVERING CHOICES

Unless you have wall-to-wall carpet or wonderful hardwood flooring that you're loathe to cover, you're going to want rugs of some sort for your home.

Before you bid on rugs at an auction, you need to know the characteristics of each type of rug—the material, the weave, the durability. Since it's impossible, at least for us, to remember every

The reverse painting on this early 1900s lamp shade, acquired at a coop, helps set the mood in our family room.

detail, it's prudent to carry a list of the salient features of various carpeting with you if you expect to be shopping for rugs. When you buy new from a carpet dealer, you have a salesperson to explain the strong and weak points of each possible selection. At an auction, the auctioneer should tell you what material a carpet is made from and the type of rug he's putting up, but after that you're on your own, and usually clueless as to whether a particular rug will suit your needs.

The following is a list of rug materials and their qualities:

ACRILAN. This bulky, very tough and durable material is a good choice for family rooms or other areas that get hard use. Moths don't like it, it's resistant to stains, and when it does become soiled it's easily cleaned.

COTTON. The pile on a cotton rug is susceptible to crushing, but the closer the weave, the less this crushing will show. Cut pile holds up better and crushes less than looped pile. Cotton rugs are not recommended for high-traffic areas.

DYNEL. Another good choice for well-used rooms, dynel is resistant to mildew, soil, and moths. It's fairly simple to clean if it does get stained.

NYLON. Although nylon doesn't resist staining quite as well as acrilan or dynel, it cleans well and wears like iron. Moths and mildew are not drawn to nylon rugs. These carpets are usually of muted colors.

RAYON. Bright, clear, soil-resistant colors are the hallmark of rayon carpets. This fabric wears well, but if the tufts aren't woven close together, the pile will crush easily.

WOOL. Some of the best carpets are made of wool. It's durable, and the colors aren't prone to fading. Many carpets are blends of wool and other materials, giving them the properties of both fabrics. A major drawback is that moths love to feast on woolen rugs. However, some wool is treated against these destructive insects.

There are several types of piles to consider. You may hear some of the following terms:

HIGH-LEVEL LOOP. In these carpets all of the loops are the same height. If the loops are close together, the carpet should hold up well in high-traffic areas of your home.

CUT PILE OR PLUSH PILE. To achieve the velvety feel of a cut or plush pile, the tops (or the loops) in the yarn are cut off evenly. These rugs are quite durable if tufts are close together.

CUT AND LOOP PILE. Looped and cut tufts are combined at varying heights, creating a sculptured look that hides footprints.

SAXONIES. Two or more pieces of yarn are twisted together, the loops are cut, and the twist is set with a heat process. You can see the twist when you look down at the individual tufts. Saxonies wear well.

With any of these weaves, if the backing is easily visible from the top of the rug, you're looking at an inferior piece of carpeting.

In addition to rug materials and weaves, there are styles of carpeting to consider. The following is a list of some rugs that commonly surface on the secondary markets:

BRAIDED RUGS. Almost always oval or round (although we have seen some oblong examples) these rugs can be hand or machine made. The original braided rugs were created from scraps of fabric left over from other sewing projects, so the colors are often random. Later, housewives purchased fabrics specifically to use for making braided rugs. The women selected the colors carefully.

Machine-made, braided rugs lack the charm of the hand-braided examples, and the low prices for which they sell reflect that. If you're considering a hand-braided rug, inspect it carefully for signs of wear and specifically for moth damage. You may find that some of the stitching that holds the braids together is broken. This is not a big deal. You can match the thread and make an easy repair.

BRUSSELS BROADLOOMS. These carpets have a hard finish that doesn't crush when it's walked on and repels dirt. They are sometimes sculptured, sometimes plain, and usually among the best buys you'll find on the secondary market.

CHENILLE BROADLOOMS. Adding a note of luxury to any environment that it graces, the chenille broadloom has the type of soft pile you can sink right into. But it's a very expensive type of carpeting and its beauty won't stand up under rough wear or harsh cleaning methods. Still, if a chenille broadloom in good condition is offered at a reasonable price, who could resist? Just realize that unless you give it a lot of TLC, it may not be your forever rug.

CHINESE RUGS. The wonderful colors in these carpets make them focal points in any rooms where they're used. Although new Chinese rugs fetch a fairly high price, you may find some very reasonable examples in the wonderful world of secondhand. Though Chinese rugs will cost you more than you'll pay for Brussels Broadlooms, if they're your taste, they're well worth the extra money. Not only are they gorgeous, they're practically indestructible.

FRENCH RUGS. The stuff dreams are made of! Lovely Aubusson, Savonnerie, etc. are so expensive they wouldn't be worth mentioning except they're too beautiful to overlook. Floral designs dominate these rugs. The Savonnerie carpets are sturdier than the Aubusson, which have a flat weave instead of the pile found in the

Savonneries. You're not likely to encounter these rugs anywhere but the finest auction houses or estate sales. Before you invest in one, be sure you know what is being offered is what it is said to be. If you don't know rugs well, have someone who is an expert take a look. You're about to spend a lot of money!

HOOKED RUGS. Hand-hooked and machine-hooked rugs set off early American or some eclectic arrangements well. Round, oval, and rectangular examples are fairly common on the secondary markets. Rose and pink on a beige background seem to be the most readily available colors. Pre-owned machine hooked rugs, especially in these colors, are sold at giveaway prices. The hand-hooked varieties bring quite a bit more, but nowhere near what the hours of labor should justify.

Hooked rugs became popular in the mid-1800s and were prevalent in the New England states. Older, more desirable examples portray a variety of scenes and patriotic themes. A family pet, a rendition of the home in which the rug was used, a bouquet of favorite flowers, or a battle scene are woven remembrances of earlier times. Hooked rugs have been manufactured for many years, too. Some of the better known makers back stamped their products. "GR," "Abenakee," and "Frost and Co" are among these marks. Any of these old rugs, either hand or machine-made are very desirable and generally sell higher than the newer hooked rugs. We think they're worth it.

If you are an animal owner, you should be aware that fine, old hooked rugs need gentle care. A rambunctious dog, or a cat intent on sharpening its claws can destroy one of these beauties in short order.

ORIENTAL RUGS. A popular preference among people who are decorating their homes, Oriental carpets are frequent offerings at auctions. In fact, there are some auctions that have nothing but Oriental rugs. Our recommendation for these specialized auctions is don't waste your time unless you want really fine carpets, are willing to pay big bucks for them, and have more than a nodding acquaintance with the intricacies of Oriental rugs. These auctions are well attended by collectors and rug dealers who know all about knots, designs, colors, and fringes. The neophyte almost never wins over the expert in these scenarios.

The subject of Oriental rugs is a complex one. People spend years studying them. We urge you not to be lured into spending a lot of money on an Oriental unless you're sure the rug is what it is touted as being. That means buying from an auctioneer or dealer whom you trust; having someone with you who can accurately appraise the rug; or being so in love with it you don't care about its real value.

Having warned you, we also want to advise you that Oriental carpets do come up at general auctions (especially those that are held to settle estates), and unless there are many of them and they've been advertised, the collectors and the dealers aren't likely to be in attendance. One rug or two just isn't enough to bring out the real rug enthusiasts. Because the competition is going to be substantially watered down, you may get an Oriental for little money.

Domestic Orientals, which are generally machine made (as opposed to the hand-tied, imported examples), are snubbed at auctions. If you have your heart set on an Oriental, consider a good quality domestic such as a Karastan. Rugs of this ilk sell for next to nothing, especially if they're put up for sale along side an imported carpet. We've seen large Karastans in beautiful condition knocked down for as little as fifty dollars!

There are a few tips that may help you attain a good Oriental. Brand new Orientals and antique Orientals are highly prized and almost always command prices that reflect this. But Orientals that are between fifty and ninety years old, while not inexpensive, often are priced within the range of people with middle-sized pocketbooks. The low thousands and sometimes even the upper hundreds could get you a gorgeous Heriz, Afshar, or Bidjar that will set the tone of a room.

There are two basic knots used in Orientals—Persian (also called Sennet) and Turkish (or Ghiordes). While both types of knots are used to produce fine Orientals, more intricate designs are possible using Persian knots.

PADDING. All rugs should be set on padding cut to fit the rug. This not only will prevent the rug from slipping or shifting, it will protect it from wear. If you're placing an area rug over wall-to-wall carpet, you'll need a thin pad that resembles a piece of sticky gauze. Pads to go directly on the floor are usually made of a cushiony rubber or a felt-like material. Sometimes rugs are sold at auctions or house sales complete with padding, but it may not be the type that's appropriate for your use. If you decide to go the secondhand route for padding, you may wait a long time before what you need appears at a sale you're attending. The problem is that an ad for an auction, tag sale, garage sale, or flea market will probably list "rugs" if there are any available, but few people will advertise padding. Instead of waiting for padding of the right size and material to surface, we suggest that if you don't get padding with a rug, you purchase what you need from a carpet store. There are a few instances when new is better. This is one of them.

WELL-DRESSED WALLS

Paint and Paper

Before you start beautifying the walls with pictures, shelving, or other artifacts, you may want to redo the walls themselves. While you're not likely to find enough wallpaper on the secondhand markets to cover an entire room, even a small one (unless you're attending an auction at a paint and paper store that's going out of business), you may encounter anywhere from one to five rolls of paper in one pattern. If you like that pattern, you can paper one wall of a room with it and paint the other three, or you may want to create panels with molding, filling in the centers with wallpaper. If there's only one roll, which won't go far, you might consider using to it to paper the back of a bookcase or china cabinet.

Whether you find wallpaper on the secondhand market, or purchase it new, there are a few rules to keep in mind: To make a room seem higher, use vertical stripes. To make a room seem longer or wider, use horizontal stripes. To make a room appear larger, either keep the walls one plain, light color or use a geometric pattern. To bring a dull room to life, try floral or botanical designs.

Although we find that cans of paint are fairly common at auctions, we avoid them, and we advise you to do the same. Unless you know how old the paint is, how it's been stored, whether or not it's been open, you're taking a real chance. With all the work that's involved with painting, why take the risk of ruining it with an inferior or even unusable product?

Deck the Walls

Art is a very personal thing. One person likes modern, another goes for the old masters, and still another would only hang the works of impressionists. There are those who think that a good print is far the best selection if you can't afford truly great originals, and those who prefer to own an original—any original because it's one of a kind. Happily, the world of secondhand can accommodate all of them.

Oil paintings are generally, but not always, worth more than water colors, acrylics, pastels, or sketches, if the quality of the work is comparable. Oils are often sold on the stretcher without a frame. But framing them needn't be costly, and they look very artsy and smart hung without frames if you have the right setting.

Most of the art you'll find at garage and yard sales is that tacky sort of commercial stuff done on some sort of pressed board or cardboard with faux brush strokes. But if you like it, you're going to get it at give-away prices. We prefer the type of art that's found at auctions. In fact, we've decked our walls with it. There are many things to consider in deciding whether or not to bid on a piece of art. First and foremost—do you like it enough to want to live with it? If the answer is "no" none of the other factors matter. You shouldn't take the picture home even if it sells for fifty cents. All art work is not created equal. There are some awful pieces that only the artist's mother could love.

Size is an important factor in establishing the price for which a piece of art will sell. A small picture generally will not sell high. Surprisingly enough, neither will an over-sized, or super-large picture. A picture that's called "sofa size" (just the right size to fit nicely over a sofa) is the most desirable and thus will bring the most money—other things being equal. And the other things are important.

Is the work original or a print? A print by a listed artist (an artist who has paintings or prints listed in one of the many art guides) or one whose works are in vogue, such as Maxfield Parrish, R. Atkinson Fox, Icart, or Wallace Nutting will fetch far more at auction than an original by an unknown—no matter how good the original may be. That's if the print is an original print—an old one. Many popular artists' and illustrators' prints have been copied. The copies are worth much less, although they're still very attractive and often in far better shape than an original print of the same picture. And why not? Most things get worn around the edges with age. Unless you're a purist, which unfortunately for our pocketbooks we are, you'll be just as happy with a reproduction print.

INSTANT RELATIVES. One of the most poignant parts of shopping the secondhand markets is viewing all the old portraits and family albums that have been discarded by relatives. We wonder how anyone could part with these jewels. The stern-looking gentlemen, the corseted ladies, the girls with huge bows and pouffy dresses, the small boys with corkscrew curls and sailor suits. They seldom sell for much at auctions and when they do, it's because the frames are desirable. We think these people from bygone days should have walls of their own, and many of them do as it becomes increasingly popular among antiques buffs to purchase the portraits of strangers and display them in their homes. These photographs are known as "instant relatives."

FRAMES. Whether a picture is framed or not will go a long way toward determining its value. But a frame that's in really bad condition can render the picture of less value than it would be if it were unframed. That's because you're going to have to replace the frame and in doing so you may find damage to the picture itself that is hidden by the frame. Of course, old ornate frames are often worth patching up with a little gesso and gold paint or gilt.

Parrish, Fox, and several other artists' prints were originally framed with pressed, molded, wooden frames, many of which have a bit of color on them. An old print of this type in its original frame is worth more than the same print in a different or newer frame, no matter how superior in quality that frame may be.

At auctions, fine old wooden frames are sold individually or in groupings. Cherry and walnut frames in a deep shadow box design are particularly sought. Gilt oak frames and frames with original art nouveau designs also are coveted. Any of these will beautify your walls. But if you're looking for inexpensive frames, you'll find them sold in box lots. Some of these frames may be broken or scratched, but there are almost always a few in good shape in any given box lot. The thin black frames that are commonly used for diplomas are frequent finds in these groups. They're ideal for framing such things as autographs, sheet music, and magazine art. Many damaged frames can be resurrected. Sometimes a coat of paint that picks up a color in the room or in the picture that's to be framed does the job. If a frame is badly scratched, sandpaper it before you paint it or cover the frame with wallpaper.

Different styles and sizes of frames used together produce an interesting display, but since the frames are diverse, this type of arrangement works best when the pictures have some relation to each other to give the display a unified look. For instance, you might select all watercolors, all floral prints, or all landscapes. Photos or small prints in similar if not identical frames give the same importance to a wall as one large picture.

What Is Art?

There are many different forms of art on both the primary and secondary markets. It's helpful to be acquainted with some of the types, and we find having knowledge makes a sale more interesting to us even if we're not buying. The following are some of the terms you're liable to encounter at sales that feature pictures:

ETCHINGS. In this process, the design or scene is eaten (called "bitten" in the art world) into a metal plate by applying acid in the appropriate places. The depressed areas are then filled with ink, the surface of the metal plate is wiped clean, and the paper is pressed on the plate hard enough to transfer the ink to the paper. Etchings are a form of *intaglio* printing, which means the design is incised into a material before being transferred.

DRY POINTS. These are similar to etchings in that they're done with the intaglio method, where the actual design is in, rather than on, a metal plate. The difference is that with dry point the design is created in needle-like points with pointed instruments rather than bitten with acid. (It looks sort of like the dot matrix done by older computer printers.) The needle-like holes are filled with ink, the plate is wiped in a blurred fashion, leaving some of the ink and resulting in a soft, muted finished product.

LIMITED EDITIONS. These are reproductions that were printed in a limited number. Most of them have a number, a slash, and another number written on them, in either pen or pencil, usually below the actual picture. The second number indicates how many pictures were printed. The first number will tell you where in the total number the print in question falls. For instance, 22/300 would indicate that three hundred prints were made and that the particular print was the twenty second one struck. Some limited editions are worth quite a bit of money, but most of them sell inexpensively once they reach the auction markets.

LITHOGRAPHS. In this process, the drawing is done with special crayons, inks, or pencils that are made from combinations of lampblack, shellac, soap, tallow, etc. The work is executed on paper, an aluminum or zinc plate, or a slab of Bavarian stone; then it's transferred to a stone or metal plate. The plate is covered with an acid that makes the design repel water and the background repel grease.

The plate is then moistened with water, which adheres to the background but is shed by the design. The next step is to roll on ink which sticks only to the dry, or design, areas. Next the paper is placed over the face plate and pressed hard so the ink will transfer.

A lithograph that has been done by the artist who created the painting is worth much more than a lithograph that's done by anyone else—if the artist is of any note. We once owned a lithograph of a black and white drawing done by the famous Mexican artist Jose Clemente Orozco. We purchased it for a few dollars at an auction where there were no art experts, had it authenticated, and sold it for about twenty times what we had paid for it.

PRINTS. Reproductions of original works of art are called prints whether they're etchings, dry points, lithographs, serigraphs, or have been reproduced by any other method.

SEPIA. A warm brown-red pigment that comes from the sac of ink found in the octopus, sepia isn't used much in modern art because it fades quickly when exposed to bright light. When a picture is called sepia, the entire work is done in a brownish tone. No other colors are used. You'll find examples of sepia art and other pictures dubbed "sepia" because of the similar color at auctions. Although they're all one tone, they're splendid additions to otherwise colorful rooms. In fact, the absence of color actually draws attention to them.

SERIGRAPHS OR SILK SCREENS. To produce a serigraph, a special type of silk is stretched on a frame so that the weave is actually pulled open. Parts of the material are then treated so liquid won't penetrate them. Each color to be used in a picture has its own silk or screen. For instance, a screen that represents red is made impervious to liquid except in the areas of the design or picture that are to be red. Paint is then forced through the open parts of the material onto paper that has been secured beneath the silk. The process is repeated for each color.

SIGNED WORKS. A print or an original with a signature is worth more if it's signed than a print or original that's unsigned *if* (and this is a big "if") the quality of the work and the reputation of the artists are comparable. If you like a picture by an "unknown"—and most of the art that's put up at auctions is by "unknowns"—by all means buy it if it's reasonable. In years to come, that artist may make a mark for himself, and you may have a valuable picture. In the meantime, you'll have a work you can enjoy.

ORIGINAL PAINTINGS. If you're contemplating spending serious money on paintings, proceed cautiously. There are many fakes in the art world. All signatures aren't authentic, and even if they are, the painting may have been "scrubbed," which means it was harshly cleaned, destroying some of the paint and in some instances going down to bare canvas. A very old painting may be cracked.

This isn't too serious if it's not too pervasive, and you probably can have it corrected by someone who repairs art. (Often, even a painting that looks like an original work may have been restored or overpainted.) A little of this is acceptable, although it will diminish the painting's value. But if the restoration is extensive it can cut the worth of the work by about three-quarters. Before you invest heavily in a painting, go over it with a black light (a special ultraviolet light which when passed slowly over a painting or object, will show any defects or new paint in a black or purple color).

POSTERS. Rolled up, framed, or mounted on cardboard, posters seem to pop up everywhere. True, most of them are pretty mundane to anyone but a teenager, but if you have an Emersonian view of seeing the world and prefer traveling by gazing at pictures and through reading books there are some that might interest you. For instance, posters depicting the Swiss Alps, a London street scene, or the Egyptian Pyramids may be perfect choices to grace your walls. There are poster-size prints of many of the works of the masters such as Cezanne, Monet, Manet, and Van Gogh, many of them were created to promote exhibitions. Some posters have a theme, such as advertising, the circus, or one of the world's fairs—these are a bit pricier.

Keep in mind the scale of your room when you're purchasing anything that's going to hang on the walls. One oversized picture or object can diminish everything else in a room and ruin your otherwise perfect decorating plans.

Other Wall Hangings

The following are some of the objects you can use to bring fun and interest to your walls inexpensively. All of them are abundant on secondary markets.

AUTOGRAPHS. If you have a home office, you might want to collect autographs of famous people, frame them, and hang them up for inspiration. This works well in a family room or music room. You can feature autographs of any famous person or if you have a specific area of interest home in on it. How about all political autographs, all sports figures—maybe musicians appeal to you more. Movie stars are a favorite and quite easy to come by. You may want all the autographs in your collection to be on letters or you may prefer that the signatures appear on pictures of the subject in question. If you patronize gourmet restaurants perhaps you'd like to frame menus signed by the various chefs. Only you can decide which autographs hold value for you.

SHEET MUSIC. Almost every antiques or collectibles outlet has at least one or two dealers who have a stack of old sheet music in their booths. The graphics on some of these are marvelous. Romantic couples, Victorian ladies, famous singers or musicians from bygone eras grace the covers. They look best framed in those narrow, black frames that we mentioned earlier. A grouping of Victorian ladies would add interest to an otherwise unspectacular hallway. And if music is your love, how about a series of sheet music covers portraying musicians? Wear and tear is sometimes a problem with old sheet music. Some bent corners can be hidden by frames, but if the music has been folded, you'll find it difficult to impossible to get rid of the crease.

MAGAZINE PICTURES. At one time years ago, we found ourselves with a half dozen lovely gold frames but no pictures to put in them. We were anxious to hang our new acquisitions so we went to a few sales where old magazines were being sold and purchased them by the stacks in the hopes of finding occupants for our frames. We intended this as a temporary solution until we found "just the right pictures" for our beautiful frames. An old cover from a popular women's magazine depicting children skating on a small pond fit into one frame. An ad for talcum powder which featured a lady with a feather boa seemed just right for another frame...and so it went, until we had all six frames filled. They looked so good, we forgot about replacing them with "just the right pictures," and we enjoyed having them hanging in our home for many years.

MIRRORS. Nothing will help you make a room look wider, deeper, or longer than a mirror. A large mirror hung opposite a window in a dark room will reflect whatever sunlight does get in and make the room about twice as light. Small mirrors, large mirrors, and medium-sized mirrors—framed or unframed—lend interest to a decorating scheme. If you hang a grouping of mirrors of various sizes sporting diverse frames on an otherwise lackluster wall, the wall will spring to life. A grouping of pictures can also be enlivened by interspersing a few mirrors in it. And, of course, the classic large mirror over a fireplace or sofa is always in style. Many old mirrors have black spots where the silvering has worn off over the years. Purists feel this only enhances the value of a mirror. We think that a few small black spots are okay, but if a mirror is too worn for our taste, we either pass it by or plan to spend the money to have it resilvered. Some glass dealers do this, but it's increasingly difficult to find them.

GREETING CARDS. Deliciously romantic old Valentine's festooned with lace or die-cut in intricate shapes are lovely subjects for framing. Cards—cute, humorous, and heart felt—framed individually or as a group—are unusual wall hangings. Greeting cards have been around since 1875 when Louis Prang started his company on the outskirts of Boston. Mr. Prang was the man who perfected colored lithography, and his pictures were of such high quality that, while the chromo process done by others has long ago deteriorated, the color in Prang's work has remained crisp and clear. A collection of Louis Prang cards is well worth having and displaying, but many of the cards done by the less famous also have charm and will be less expensive. Greeting cards, unlike postcards, aren't a particularly popular collectible. We've been at auctions where no one except us, including the auctioneer, ever heard of Louis Prang. When this happens you can get marvelous buys.

PLATES. The commemorative plates that sell new for upwards of $35 glut the secondhand markets and, with rare exception, bring less than a third of their original selling price. Bing and Grondahl, Royal Copenhagen, Norman Rockwell, and Hummel plates bring the most money. And some of those that go back to the late 1800s and early 1900s do sell high. But there are times when even the most desirable plates sell at auctions or flea markets for well under $10. An arrangement of plates in colors you find pleasing may be the solution for a spot on your living room or dining room wall. Some people prefer the blue and white Bing and Grondahl or Royal Copenhagen plates. Others will hang only the Hummels. And Norman Rockwell has a devoted following many of whom select plates to which they can relate. For instance, someone with children might only want plates that depict kids doing ordinary kid things.

Other plates make attractive wall arrangements, too. Some of the hand painted plates done in the many porcelain factories in Limoges, France are in themselves works of art. During the late 1800s and early 1900s, painting porcelain blanks was a popular hobby for women. Most of them signed and dated the pieces on which they'd worked. Surprisingly, many of these women had artistic talent and their art work is well executed. Some of the plates don't have a factory mark on them. These unsigned blanks were usually of inferior quality, but that doesn't mean that the artist didn't have superior talent. Some of the plates have two backstamps—one from the factory that made the blank and another from a different factory where the decoration was done. Plates that were hand painted at a factory are the ones that sell highest. The assumption is that since the artists were professionals, their work is better—not always true. Painting that was done at a factory is almost always under glaze, making it easy to distinguish from that done by amateurs.

Planning Your Walls

ARRANGEMENTS. After you have all the right pictures or objects that you think will dress up a wall or room, actually hanging them can seem daunting. How do you know they'll look the way you envision them? What if you hang them and they don't look right? Not to worry. There are ways to avoid making needless holes in your pristine walls.

Our favorite way of doing this is to put a piece of brown wrapping paper, about the size of the wall area we're planning to decorate, on the floor—preferably in front of the wall on which we're going to hang them. Then we take the pictures, plates, mirrors, or whatever we want to use on that area and arrange them on the paper until we're satisfied with them. We try them every which way. It's okay because we're not making holes in the walls. When we get them the way we want them, and we've exactly measured the spaces between what we're about to hang, we use these measurements to guide us as we put the pictures on the wall.

Our second favorite method is to affix the brown paper to the wall, either with tape or small tacks, then cut out cardboard in the shapes of the objects to be hung. Tape these on the brown paper until you have a pleasing arrangement, trace around the shapes on the paper, and cut them out. Lightly trace the outlines you've created in stencil form on the brown paper onto the wall, using a pencil. Remove the brown paper from the wall and hang the pictures or other items in their assigned spaces. You may have to fill in the nail holes you made hanging the paper; but if you're hanging a large group of pictures, it's worth the extra work.

The third system is to cut the shapes of the objects out of cardboard or paper, and hang them on the wall with double sided tape. You can move them around until you've found just the arrangement that you want. When we tried this, we found that when the tape was removed, part of our new paint job came with it. Perhaps it was because the paint was too new; but, though we know people who swear this is the best way, we've never tried it again.

LIGHTING

You'll find a dazzling assortment of gently (and not so gently) used lighting fixtures are available on the secondhand markets. Many of the buys are spectacular—so spectacular that without careful planning, you may end up with great buys of the wrong type of illumination for your needs. Most auctions offer some lamps and other light fixtures and many of them are almost giveaways, so you can afford to be selective and still get what you want without having to wait for months.

A Light for Every Purpose

There are four basic categories of illumination that should interest you. *Task Lighting* is needed to cast light that's bright enough for work or reading. *Ambient Lighting* usually comes from an overhead light and provides a friendly spot for conversation or for watching television but not bright enough for close work. *Indirect Lighting* can bounce off of mirrors, ceilings, floors, and walls and is often used in conjunction with ambient lighting to brighten a room. Indirect lighting makes a room seem larger than it is, especially if the walls are a light color that picks up and reflects the light. *Accent Lighting* is used to show off a particular spot or item such as a picture, a piece of sculpture or a display of collectibles. We have seen accent lights used innovatively in cabinets, or shining up from the floor onto an object rather than down from the ceiling.

Assessing Your Needs

Ambient and indirect lighting add a warm glow to any room, but too many task lights or accent lights create the feeling of confusion by featuring too many items or sections of a room. They can also cause a nasty glare if they reflect in a mirror or the glass on a print. The kitchen is an exception to this. You need good visibility in all the work areas of this room. Cabinets, pot racks, and appliances cast shadows that can interfere with your ability to see what you're doing. Fluorescent lights installed under the cabinets brighten up counters and other work areas, making food preparation much easier. And a bright, hanging light with bulbs that shine down rather than upwards does wonders over a kitchen island. Depending on the size of the room, you may also want ambient lighting. Both fluorescent lights and appropriate hanging lights appear with regularity at auctions, garage sales, and flea markets for pennies on the dollar of what you'd pay for them new.

Bathrooms also need good light. It's difficult to apply makeup or shave without it. The light should be directed so that it shines on the *person*, and not on the mirror. Fixtures placed over mirrors are common. In order to do the job, they should be a minimum of two-feet long and consist of fluorescent tubes or rows of bulbs. Wall-mounted fixtures on both sides of a mirror are probably the best choice if the mirror is small (about the size you'll find on a standard medicine cabinet). The light coming from both sides illuminates a person's entire face.

Bedrooms need multipurpose lights. The lighting by a mirror needs to be bright enough to show up the same realities that sunlight reveals. Dim mood lighting is attractive in a bedroom, too. You'll need reading lamps beside your bed. If you select those that have narrow points of light, instead of lamps with wide shades that fan out the light, one partner can read while the other sleeps undisturbed.

Living rooms and family rooms lend themselves to all forms of lighting, although ambient lighting has fallen from favor for living room use in the past few decades. Home-fashion decorators do change their minds. A few years ago, it was considered tacky not to have two matching lamps on two matching tables flanking a sofa. We think the current trend toward different lamps is much more inviting. But do remember when you begin your search for lamps that are to be used near each other, they should be close enough in height and shape to balance. A tall, thin lamp on one end table and a short, squat one on the other just doesn't work. If the lamps on your end tables are intended to be reading lights, the bottoms of the shades should be at about one-inch below eye-level when you're seated beside the lamp.

A Perfect Plan

Before you start your search for lighting, make a plan of your home, marking spaces for lights and noting the types that will best fit those spaces. Take into account your needs for each room—doing homework takes task lighting, watching television doesn't. And pay attention to the height you'll want in your lamps. (A light that shines in your eyes because it's too tall isn't a plus.) Having a fairly firm idea of your lighting needs will eliminate the necessity to do fast thinking about whether you want a certain lamp, sconce, or chandelier, when it comes up for sale. Split second decisions are often ones that we regret later.

PUTTING THE PLAN TO WORK. When you get to a sale, look over any lighting fixture well for chips, cracks, or crazing. If these are in inconspicuous places, you may get yourself a spectacular buy. If there is a shade or shades, take a close look. If they're dirty, try brushing the dust off. Is the material washable? Do they look like they can be brought back to life? If the fixture itself is brass or copper and has a sort of patchy appearance, it probably was coated with a sealer which has started to wear off. While sealers keep brass looking bright and polished for a long time, the down side of them is that when the sealers start to wear off, you're left with the problem of removing the remaining sealer. This can't be done with brass polish. It takes work and lots and lots of elbow grease, combined with a semi-abrasive product.

Often a pair of lamps is available at a yard sale, flea market, or auction and one is in beautiful shape while the other is badly damaged. Don't let this deter you from buying them if you like the good one and it will fit into your home. You can keep the damaged lamp for parts. Perhaps the harp or the shade are worth salvaging. Even if after looking over a pair of lamps you find the best of the pair has a small chip in the back or other inconspicuous place, you can still make use of it. That small imperfection is going to turn off all the folks who won't buy anything unless it's perfect—and that means most dealers.

Speaking of "perfect condition," old lamps, and even newer ones, often have unsafe wiring. We almost always rewire light fixtures before we use them, and we urge you to do the same—especially with a lamp that has a cloth cord. The harp on a lamp may be bent. You can either bend it back into shape or replace it, which isn't a big deal. If you don't luck out and find lamps with shades in good condition, there are several ways to go. If the frame of the shade is good, you may want to cover it with fabric or parchment paper. (There are many good books that give instructions on how to do this.) If the shade just looks tired, you may want to paint it or make a collage on it. If the shade's a total loss, you can look at other sales for shades—they come up frequently. If all else fails, you'll find fairly inexpensive shades at department stores that carry lower-priced merchandise.

FLOOR LAMPS. In addition to table lamps, you may need a couple of torchiers or other floor lamps. They're ideal for spots where you need light but either don't want or don't have room for a table. Floor lamps are also more versatile than table lamps because they're easy to move to a place where you want light on a temporary basis, such as beside a card table where you're playing a game or doing a puzzle. They won't take up part of your table surface.

SCONCES. With sconces you can add a formal or informal note to a room depending on the design of the light fixtures. Their versatility makes sconces good candidates for use in a dining room, hall, bedroom, or over a mantle. Some are made to hold candles—others are electrified or burn oil or kerosene. This form of indirect lighting can be very dramatic. We have friends who bought a pair of art deco sconces at auction for just a few dollars. They must have been long abandoned because they were filthy and covered with flecks of black paint. Once the paint was removed, the glass washed and shined, and the sconces rewired, our friends installed them over a buffet in their dining room. The rays of light beaming toward the ceiling brought the entire room to life. And the best part is they got these treasures for a throw-away price.

CHANDELIERS. Real show-stoppers in the lighting department, we particularly like chandeliers in a master bedroom where they add a romantic touch. But because chandeliers are so commanding that they can overlight and overpower most rooms, we think they should always be on dimmer switches, especially in a bedroom where soft lighting helps set a mood.

CREATIVE CONVERSIONS. In your search for lighting, let your imagination take over. Many objects that were never fashioned to be electric lamps can be converted with little effort. Old oil and kerosene lamps were, of course, made to provide light and some purists want to keep them as they were intended to be. Other people prefer to electrify them figuring that they're safer, and, unless the electricity goes off, more useful.

Statues also can be fashioned into attractive lamps. Years ago, we bought a large replica of Rebecca at the Well at an auction. When we got it home the statue seemed to be a bit too large for our living room. Then we had the bright idea to make it into a lamp to go on a table beside a fairly large chair. A thin piece of tubing, some wiring, a harp (which we had on hand from another old lamp), and a shade (which we also found at auction) and we had a one-of-a-kind conversation piece to light up a corner of our room.

This brass chandelier was dark with age and splattered with paint when we bought it; but all five shades were perfect. We're pleased with the results of our cleaning, polishing, and rewiring efforts.

Another time we found two signed, French statues at a flea market. Immediately we both thought of them as possible lamps for our bedroom. It was the end of the day and the vendor was anxious to sell them, so he settled for a very low price. We wired them, and must admit we bought new, silk shades (which cost about ten times what we'd paid for the statues). They still flank our bed.

Innovative people have made lamps from any number of items that were originally designed for other purposes. Coffee grinders, high button shoes (first filled with concrete), vases, sad irons, clocks—a host of unseemly articles can be made into lamps with wiring, inexpensive parts from a hardware store, and a little imagination.

LIGHT BULBS. The light bulbs you select will subtly change the mood of a room. Of course, the wattage is important, but there are other considerations, too. Plain glass can be harsh and evoke a business-like, no-nonsense feeling. They're often the best choice for task lighting, especially if the task is a finicky one and you need to see every detail clearly. Using frosted light bulbs softens that look, giving a more relaxed ambiance. Pink bulbs create warmth, love, romance, friendship. They make happy rooms. Blue and green bulbs, which aren't as easy to find as the others, turn a room from hot to cool and are good choices for indirect lighting when the weather is sizzling.

Searching the secondhand markets, you'll find enough lights for your entire house, and you should get them for less than the price you'd pay for one good lamp at retail. That's real savings.

WINDOWS ON THE WORLD

Should you accentuate windows, dress them to match the walls; or simply frame them, allowing the view to garner the attention? That's a multi-faceted decision and depends on the type of room you want to create and the appearance of your windows. You'll also want to take into consideration whether you have a panoramic view, your window overlooks an alley, or the truth lies somewhere in between. Privacy will be another factor. Do you want a window arrangement that keeps the outdoors out? If so you'll need draw drapes, shades, or Venetian blinds. Perhaps you don't want a clear view but would like to let in some light. In that case, perhaps sheer or semi-sheer curtains are for you. If you go that route, you may want sheers that match the color of your walls or you may opt for light enhancing white. You may want to set off your sheers with drapes or some sort of side curtain.

The Long and Short of It

A rule of thumb—but, certainly not a rule written in stone—is that long curtains or drapes are for formal rooms, while short ones are for informal rooms. You'll need exact measurements to buy intelligently. You can shorten drapes or curtains that are too long, but if yours is a room that needs a long treatment, purchasing examples that are too short can sabotage your entire plan. Unfortunately, most secondhand sales are of the "now-or-never type." By the time you've gone home to measure, the drapes will likely be sold. The answer is to measure your windows *before* you go looking. You need the width, the length from where you'll be hanging curtains or drapes above the window to the floor, to the baseboard, to the sill, and to the bottom of the wooden part beneath the sill (called the apron). Any other lengths won't look well. These are standard. There is an exception, however, if the bottom half of the drape or curtain will be hidden behind a sofa or other solid piece of furniture, no one is going to see it, so it doesn't really matter how long or short it is, provided the bottom doesn't show. In a bed and breakfast where we once stayed, the lace curtains in our room cascaded down the sides of the window and pooled on the floor. The extra length of material was very dramatic. (Another rule successfully broken!)

Setting the Tone

The window treatment you select should reflect the style of your room. If the curtains or drapes are your first purchase, you can use them as a jumping off point for decorating the rest of the room. If you've already selected other pieces, especially upholstered pieces, you need to consider them when you consider window dressing. Windows can be the focal point of a room or serve as a background for your other furnishings. Straight, no-nonsense curtains and drapes are the most prevalent both on the primary and secondary markets—perhaps because there is less work in making them and so they're less expensive. These window treatments lend themselves to all styles of decorating, but the fabrics and colors in which they're found don't necessarily go with everything, and must be considered so that style, fabric, and color all complement each other and your room.

Sheer curtains add a light, soft, feminine touch to a room. If they have ruffles, they're a good choice for bedrooms or for an unsophisticated room, but they don't work well in formal rooms. Curtains of bold plaids and stripes, coarse homespun materials, and rough textures create a masculine, or informal, atmosphere. They're excellent choices for a man's study, a family room, or a game room.

Floor-length, tailored, straight curtains or drapes with pinch pleats at the top set off a formal setting. The room will look even more formal if the walls are white and the drapes a dark color or if the walls are a dark color and the drapes are white, but this startling contrast, especially with darker walls, will make the room appear smaller than it is.

Window Strategy

You may wish to have windows that don't call attention to themselves. This can be achieved with drapes that match the color of plain walls or with drapes and wallpaper in the same colors and pattern. Small rooms appear larger when the curtains are part of the background. If you go this route, we strongly advise you to get your drapes first. If you paint your walls in advance, you're in for a difficult time finding curtains or drapes to match. Even if you buy drapes new, you'll find colors are limited. But it seems that there's an almost limitless number of paint colors from which to choose.

Patterned drapes will provide you with a color scheme. Pick out one of the colors in the pattern for your walls and other colors for your upholstered furnishings. The match between walls and the color in the drapes doesn't have to be as exact as it needs to be if both the walls and the curtains are the same plain color. Unless your room is an especially large one, avoid busy patterns. They create a feeling of restlessness on an area as large as the average window if the room is small. Curtains of a sunny color bring a dreary room to life. Keeping colors the same value or intensity is important, too. You don't want to add Chinese red drapes, no matter how magnificent they are, to a room of gentle pastels.

Most of the more modern windows are made from Low-E glass which substantially cuts down on fabrics fading. However, many of us in older homes don't have this modern convenience, and keeping our valued drapes, rugs, and upholstery from fading is still of paramount concern. Sheers and semi-sheers don't seem to do an adequate job of this, so for sunny windows we recommend either venetian blinds, full shades, or drapes that can be kept closed to keep out the light during the sunny hours. Dark drapes in a sunny window will fade, even if they're fade-resistant. We recommend that you use liners or, at the very least, lined drapes to keep the problem to a minimum. On one of our windows we hung white sheets on the same drapery hooks from which our red velvet drapes hung. They worked well. The drapes came from an estate sale; the sheets came from a garage sale. The total cost was minimal.

A sepia print of Cleopatra adds interest to this otherwise plain wall.

Necessity is the Mother of Many Window Treatments

The recycled items available on the secondhand markets that can be used on windows don't stop with curtains and drapes. Some of the most interesting windows are dressed with items that were never intended to be used in this manner. When is a bedspread not a bedspread? When some inventive person has used a pair of scissors and needle and thread to turn it into a pair of drapes. There are boxes of bedspreads at auctions, especially estate auctions, where all the spreads in the house are often lumped together and sold as one lot. Wow! Two twin spreads can easily be made into a pair of curtains or drapes by putting a heading on them, hemming them, and hanging them. It's that simple. Some large and truly exquisite spreads are discarded because they have a spot, a cigarette burn, or show wear in the middle—right where it would show on a bed. But take that spread, cut the fabric in three pieces—the third piece being the middle, from top to bottom, cutting out the offending area—and the other two pieces will make perfect drapes for a window. Of course, all this depends on the material used in the spread and whether or not you like it and if it will fit into your home decor.

We've also seen an old log cabin design quilt used as a one-piece drape that opened to one side of a patio door (just as many drapes made for a patio do). This unique drape looked just right in the home, which was full of primitive and country style furnishings. And the best part is that this smart lady didn't destroy the quilt, or lessen its value, by using it this way.

The fabric from an old table cloth can be converted to a curtain—usually for a small window—with a little work. Or you might come across a tablecloth that's badly and permanently stained, but that sports a border of lovely old lace. Most people spurn a cloth like this, but you can remove the lace and use it to trim curtains for your bedroom or dining room. Satin sheets provide another possible material for curtains. We were in a home recently that had towels for curtains in the guest bathroom. The towels were hung by rings pinned through the material—no sewing required.

Wallpaper borders create a decorative splash when they're used around the molding of a window. Many lots that are too small to do a room but large enough to do a window can often be found at estate auctions or garage sales. This is a good way to treat a window if you want maximum light. Adding a shade or venetian blind will fill your need for privacy at night. Venetian blinds, still in their boxes, frequently turn up at sales. They're not big sellers because most people don't roam the sales armed with a list of needed measurements. But you will!

Finding the Real Thing

Of course, there are many legitimate curtains and drapes out there. Look for fading, especially on the edges, before you consider purchasing them. If the drape is large and your window is small, the fading might not matter. Perhaps you can cut the curtain down and get rid of this discoloration. If the material is truly beautiful (as it is in many drapes) but much of it is faded, worn, or unusually dirty, look it over with an eye to possibly getting enough material from it to make a pillow.

You can use short curtains or drapes that don't fit any of your windows by hanging two pairs on a fairly large window—one over the top half of the window and the other over the bottom half in cafe style. This gives an informal and, depending on the material, a cottage-atmosphere to a room.

What to do if you have a wide window and all the drapes you find are gorgeous but too narrow? If there are several of them, consider sewing together enough of them until you have two panels of a width that will cover your window. This is really easy. Even if you hardly know which end of a needle to use, you can baste the panels together and no one will ever know the difference. When we went through our "ruffles-in-the-bedroom" stage, we found just the right curtains—lovely sheers with wide ruffles in the middle and ruffled tiebacks. But although they were the right length, they were nowhere near wide enough. However, there were two pairs and we had only one window to consider. The solution: we used both pairs, putting one panel on each side the way it was supposed to go, with the ruffles meeting in the middle, and the other pair inside out on the ends of the rod, so that a ruffle was also at the edge of the window. Then we added the tiebacks. It was a generous enough fit so that there was no need to sew the curtains together—the place where they met was masked by the folds.

The Importance of Fabric

At sales, you're going to find ready made curtains and drapes, but you'll also find bolts of material that might be used for dressing windows. If you're considering fabric, look it over for flaws and scrunch a piece together, holding it up so it will hang in folds as it would in a curtain or drape. A fabric will look quite different in soft folds than it does on a bolt.

The weave is important, too, when you assess material as a potential window treatment. Open weaves are less formal than tighter, closer ones. There are two kinds of threads in weaving: The filling threads, which are put on a loom or machine first. These are the threads into which the other type of threads—the warp threads—are woven. Following is a brief description of some of the more common weaves:

PLAIN WEAVE. As the name implies, this is the simplest of all weaves, and it's a strong one. Single warp threads are alternately passed over and under the filling threads. Calico, chintz, linen, taffeta, and voile are examples of plain weave materials that are suitable for window treatments.

BASKET WEAVE. Although this is a variation of the plain weave, it doesn't make as strong a material. To produce a basket weave, more than one warp thread is passed under and over a corresponding number of filling threads. For example, if four warp threads are bunched together they will be woven in and out of bunches of four filling threads. Monks cloth is probably the best example of a basket weave.

TWILL. This weave is done by weaving the warp thread through the filling thread in an over-and-under motion diagonally instead of horizontally as in the basket weave or plain weave. Denim, which can be used for curtains or drapes in a child's room, has a twill weave. Satin is a variation of twill.

PILE WEAVE. This weave often is used in material for carpets or upholstery. There are two sets of warp threads. These aren't bunched together as the warp threads are in a basket weave. One is for the body of the fabric; the other is for the loops on top of the body of the fabric. Sometimes the loops are trimmed, as with velvet, which makes luxurious drapes in a formal room.

GAUZE WEAVE. The filler threads are put on the loom or machine and then two warp threads are twisted around each other with a filler thread in the middle of each loop formed by the twisted warp thread. Marquisette is an example of this weave. It's good for lightweight curtains.

Tips on Hanging Window Treatments

After your drapes are sewn, washed, ironed, or whatever you need to do to make them right for your windows, you'll be faced with the problem of hanging them. If you've been alert at the sales, you've probably got the proper rods and hardware for this task. These things are certainly out there.

If you're hanging sheers and overdrapes, you can either use a rod that's made to accommodate both, use two separate rods (one over the other), or hang the sheers inside the window frame, in which case you won't have to use as deep a rod as you will if you're using two rods that protrude into the room. Spring-loaded rods work well inside a window frame.

If the absence of light is a problem in your room or if you just want to take advantage of the entire view, try hanging drapes far enough out from the edges of the window so that when the drapes are open, the window is completely uncovered. Be sure you hang the rods from a stud, or the first time you pull your drapery cord, the entire rod may come tumbling down.

Accessorizing Your Windows

With windows, as with many things in life, little things make a big difference. They're the extra touches that turn an ordinary window dressing into an extraordinary one. Crystals or stained glass pieces, either of which are common finds in the secondhand markets, are examples of this. Other extra additions also can be used to liven up a bland window treatment.

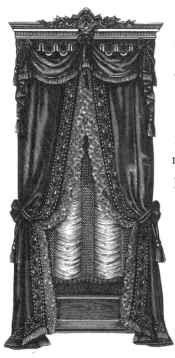

VALANCES. Whether they're wooden, made of draped material, or constructed of some other fabric, valances give a finished look to a window, but if they're not in proper scale, they also can overpower the room. If your room is informal, select valances with clean simple lines, and don't make them any wider or higher than they need to be to cover the hardware and tops of drapes and curtains. On the other hand, valances can be quite elaborate and detailed in a formal room, especially if the room is a large one.

From a box lot of draperies, you may find that you have more of any one design than you need. If you already have wooden valances, consider covering them with the material from those that are left over. It's not difficult. You can pull the material over the wood, stapling it on the back or, if you're gifted in working with fabric, you can pad the front of the valance to give it a more detailed, three-dimensional appearance. A valance painted the same color as the drapes, or a contrasting color, ties your whole window treatment together, too. Taking an extra drapery panel and draping it on metal corner pieces makes an attractive and ultra-easy valance.

TIE BACKS. Gathering curtains and drapes back lets in light and is especially popular with the use of under curtains made of sheer fabrics. There are many handsome metal tie backs on the secondary markets now—some are quite ornate. Many times we've purchased them still in their unopened packages at garage sales and flea markets. Tie backs made from the same material as the drapes or curtains are less formal than the metal tie backs or the fancy tassels which add a Victorian touch to a room.

Curtains and drapes are only one part of the total of a room, but they're a very important part. They dress up your own, personal windows on the world.

CHAPTER THREE

How to Buy Furniture: The Basics

EVERYTHING OLD beomes new again—to the buyer. And if you've never shopped in the used furniture markets before, we believe you're going to have new and exciting experiences searching for used furniture. In our humble opinions, new furniture stores are sterile and fatuous, while used-furniture markets are ripe with mystery and adventure. Better yet, the array of furniture styles available in the used market is virtually unlimited. What's more, searching for a particular piece in the used market may not take any longer than hunting for it in new furniture stores. Of course, a lot depends on luck—and how precisely you've set your target. Here's a recent experience of ours that illustrates the point:

A few months prior to this writing we decided to replace our living room arm chairs. We'd picked up a matching pair at a garage sale only a year earlier. They're beautiful, quality-constructed chairs in like-new condition, and their color and style

An example of a fairly modern, very solid wood kitchen set priced on the secondhand market at a fraction of the cost of its newer counterparts.

harmonize with the room's traditional decor. Placed on each side of the fireplace, they looked, in our opinions, terrific. But they had one flaw, they're not comfortable enough for either of us to sit for an entire evening. And we're accustomed to spending winter evenings sitting by the fireplace.

We endured this situation for several months, trying to adjust to the "new" chairs, until one day we both got fed up and decided to go out and buy comfortable chairs, immediately—no waiting for an auction, no roaming flea markets and garage sales, no secondhand shops. We set out to visit new furniture stores and select the perfect pair of chairs. We knew it would cost more, but we figured it would be the fastest and most efficient way to bring home comfortable chairs—besides, we owed it to our backs!

Ha! After a three-week search of every furniture store within a radius of fifty miles of our home, we came up with a big fat zero. We couldn't find chairs that combined the style, size, comfort, and quality we were looking for. In addition to that, the chairs were either sleazy or unbelievably expensive—sometimes both! And if we found what we wanted, delivery could take up to six months. We were disappointed and frustrated.

About two weeks after we gave up looking in new furniture stores, we spotted a wing chair in an antiques shop. It bore the label of an upscale manufacturer and had just been reupholsterd. Everything about the chair was first class. We both sat in it and it seemed comfortable. The dealer agreed to come down $80. We went outside and discussed the pros and cons. The only possible con was comfort. So we went back in and took turns lounging in the chair for about fifteen minutes and still found it comfortable. During this time, the dealer showed remarkable patience and good humor. We closed the deal—paying about a fourth of the price of a new one—and have been happy with our purchase ever since.

Ah, but there is more. A few weeks later we found the identical chair, same good label and everything, but with different fabric, at a garage sale and bought it for even less money. The fabric color isn't quite right, so we plan to recover it eventually. The chair was a splendid buy, we're pleased with it, and can enjoy comfortable evenings in our living room once again thanks to the secondary markets.

Incidentally, the original pair of matching arm chairs are still in our living room, still beautiful, and comfortable for any guests without back problems.

Auctions are another fine place to look for furniture. The dining room set we own, and are very proud of, was purchased at auction. Ours was the only bid on this gorgeous, almost new (no visible wear) Henredon table with two extensions leaves and six chairs upholstered in a rose stripe that goes beautifully with our wallpaper. Identical sets retail for about $4,000. And we got it for...are you sitting down?...the incredible sum of $200. What a deal—what a steal! After the sale we analyzed our stroke of good luck and decided that the furniture dealers weren't interested in the set because it was too new, it didn't have a china closet, and the table is incredibly heavy. It cost us $25 to have the set delivered, and the guys who had to carry it complained bitterly about the heft of the table. An additional $25 as a tip brought smiles all around, and we had our dining room set. Some new furniture stores offer free delivery in their local area; others charge around $35 or more.

GETTING STARTED: FORM VS. FUNCTION

Before you hit the trail for furniture, there are a few basic things you should know. Actually, what follows includes a lot of just-common-sense suggestions you may already be aware of. But it's worth reviewing so the information will be readily available when you need it. We hope you'll also find useful tips here that are new to you and will prepare you to shop wisely.

To begin with, it's difficult, if not down-right impossible, to furnish your house or apartment with furniture you'll love and enjoy for many years to come if you don't know what styles are available. For most people, furniture has two functions: to supply a resting place for their bodies or possessions, and to provide an esthetic quality to their living space. In other words, the norm is to seek furniture that is both utilitarian and attractive.

In addition, durability is highly desirable. That is, your furniture pieces should remain sturdy and functional for a lifetime or more—and they will, if they're not abused. True, in time wood surfaces may need to be refinished, joints tightened or re-glued, and upholstery refurbished with new padding and fabric. However, in most cases, reconditioning a quality piece of furniture is far less expensive than replacing it with a new one. So in order to buy durable furniture, you need to know some elementary facts about furniture construction.

Just as individual tastes change in clothing, food, entertainment, and so on, they change with furnishings, so it's important to know what your tastes are now if you want to satisfy them. If you don't know what's available, or haven't given thought to what styles of furniture you find appealing, the odds are against your coming home with a piece you'll be happy with for a long time. Have you ever made a purchase and a few days or weeks later found that item in a color or style you much prefer? We have.

To guarantee satisfaction in your purchase, your first step is to determine what style of furniture you want. Look everywhere! Look in books, in magazines, in catalogs, in stores, in friends houses, in movies and on TV shows. Look at the over-all style of the rooms. Look at the furniture arrangements. And look at individual pieces.

Beauty is in the eye of the beholder—that's why there are so many styles of furniture. However, there are only two basic furniture styles: traditional or period and modern. To the novice, period styles are difficult to distinguish, and rightly so. Many styles are only variations of the preceding period. But many styles are quite different, so if you are interested in period furnishings, it's a good idea to learn, or write down, the names of the styles you like for further reference. Remember, you're not limited to one style, you can mix them and create your own eclectic style. In fact, mixing styles is the best way to add interest and your personal stamp on a room. The same is true of modern styles—mix them for a one-of-a-kind room look. Mixing period and modern furniture can also be successfully done. Often just one piece—a chest, a chair, or perhaps a table—with contrasting lines will liven up an otherwise bland room.

Once furniture has been used, even if only for a very short period of time, it's secondhand and will command only second-hand prices. But if it's old enough to be considered antique (*and that doesn't mean the 100-year definition used by some people*) then the sky is the limit as to what it will bring on the market. At this point in time, 1950s furniture and accessories are just beginning to be considered collectible. This means that if you like the 1950s styling, you may be able to get good buys on what in another few years will be worth a great deal more money. However, our advice is not to buy anything you don't like just because you think it's a good investment. The market is fickle and you could get burned.

If you're starting from scratch to furnish a home rather than re-furnishing it (which you can do at your leisure), you may feel overwhelmed. Dividing the overall job into small projects should help relieve the stress. The first thing to do is make a list of the absolute essentials. You're going to need a bed on which to sleep, a table and chairs for comfortable eating, and a chair and/or sofa in which to relax. If you're taste runs to legitimate period pieces, you'll be making more of a cash outlay than you will if you're satisfied with more contemporary pieces.

When Not to Buy Secondhand

A few items are quite risky to get secondhand, and mattresses and box springs count among them. In most states, secondhand mattresses and box springs are not supposed to be sold unless they've been treated (actually fumigated). This doesn't mean that really gross mattresses aren't sold at garage sales and flea markets. It's just that auctioneers are generally a bit more conscientious in fulfilling the law. And at many sales, to comply with the letter of the law, a mattress and box spring will be "given away" with the purchase of the bed. *If at all possible, we advise you buy a new mattress and box spring.*

If you're really strapped financially, look for your mattress and box springs at either an estate auction or at a tag sale where you can actually see the bedding set up and may get an opportunity to try them out for comfort.

Below are brief descriptions of major furniture styles. Hopefully, they will aid you in sifting through the classified ads and auction catalogs with the ability to recognize what is listed.

A GALLERY OF FURNITURE STYLES

ITALIAN RENAISSANCE. Made in Italy between the 14th and 17th centuries, this is heavy, rectangular furniture made of dark walnut. The decoration is grandly carved in intricate designs. Upholstery is thick and sumptuous.

ELIZABETHAN. Made in England from 1558 to 1603, and named for Elizabeth I, this is heavy rectangular furniture of oak, elaborately carved. The legs usually feature large, carved balls. This is not a delicate or refined style.

FRENCH RENAISSANCE. Large, heavily carved pieces of oak, French Renaissance was made in France between 1558 and 1625. The carving is superior to that of English furniture of that period.

JACOBEAN, EARLY. A style similar to Elizabethan, but with less ornate carvings, that was made in England from 1603 to 1660. It has a dark stained finish.

Because this cherished pine desk was made by an amateur craftsman and isn't very old, $75 made it ours. Notice the unusual carving on the back of the chair. The moriage vase, the Victorian clock, the Italian jewelry box, and the horse bookend (sans mate) all came in box lots.

LOUIS XIII. Greatly influenced by the Italian renaissance, this style of furniture was made in France from 1610 until 1643. Spiral legs are common, and the chairs are low-backed.

COLONIAL. A term popularly used to describe any furniture made in the American colonies prior to the revolution, we use the term to include only furniture made from 1625 until 1689. Oak was the wood of choice, and grooved stiles (vertical frame), rails, and carved panels were commonly used.

LOUIS XIV. A heavy, rectangular furniture with straight lines, this style was made in France from 1643 until 1715. Dark wood was used until late in the period when lighter colored woods were introduced. Most pieces have under braces and are so heavy that they are difficult to move.

JACOBEAN, LATE. This furniture appeared during the years referred to as the Restoration Period. Made in England between 1660 and 1688, it shows a strong influence of Italian baroque and is ornate with scrolls, lacquered ornamentation, and gilt.

PAINTED ITALIAN. Raised designs of gesso (a mixture of plaster of Paris and glue) distinguish this furniture. Often made of cheap wood, the pieces are beautifully painted with designs and/or scenes—sometime by leading artists of the time. Legs and arms are curved, and many pieces have a *bombe* (curved outward) front. Made in Italy from 1680 until 1820.

NEO-CLASSIC. Eighteen and 19th centuries style of simplicity, symmetry, and order inspired by classic Greek and Roman design.

AMERICAN COUNTRY. Rustic pieces with simple lines made by rural cabinet makers in this country from 1690 to 1890. Common pieces are Boston rockers, slat back chairs, wagon seats, trestle tables, dry sinks, and corner cupboards.

QUEEN ANNE. Most often made of solid walnut or other woods topped with a walnut veneer, this style was produced in England from 1702 until 1714 and in America from 1725 to 1750. Its delicate curved lines usually included cabriole legs (S shaped, swelling out at the knee and inward at the ankle) and club feet or ball-and-claw feet. Shell ornamentation was amply used.

REGENCE. Made in France, from 1715 to 1723, this style has more curves and fewer rectangles than earlier styles. The pieces are of a modest size, with small decorations, and often made of metal. (Note: The English Regency spelling ends with a "y".)

LOUIS XV. This small, light, and highly decorated style was made in France from 1723 to 1774. Decorations consist of inlay, gilding, polychroming (many colors), or artistic painting. Chests often have bombe (bulging) fronts.

CHIPPENDALE, ENGLISH. Produced in England from 1749 until 1779, Chippendale chairs, tables, and cabinets have carved aprons and skirts. The legs are usually cabriole and the wood mahogany. The finish is stained dark.

CHIPPENDALE, AMERICAN. Made in America between 1755 and 1799, this style features either cabriole legs with ball-and-claw feet or straight, square legs. The fronts of the chests and desks have bowed serpentine or oxbow fronts. Most of this style furniture was made of mahogany.

ADAMS. This style has an architectural appearance with its straight, rectangular structure. It was made in England from 1760 until 1793 and has classical motifs painted by skilled artists and upholstery of elegant fabrics such as silk. Most pieces are made of mahogany.

A pair of Victorian chairs and a pie crust table are the highlights of this conversation spot in front of one of the twin fireplaces in this home.

LOUIS XVI. Produced in France from 1774 to 1793, this style is smaller and more delicate than Louis XV. It has straight, rectangular lines with tapered legs. The pieces are often painted and decorations are minimal.

HEPPLEWHITE. Created in England from 1780 to 1795, it has small, graceful, straight lines with slender legs—sometimes ending with small, spade feet (tapered with four sides). Oval, shield, or hoop chair backs were featured. Mahogany was generally the wood of choice, and marquetry (a geometrical-patterned veneer) often enhanced the graceful design.

FEDERAL. Not a distinct furniture style, but a type of ornamentation that reflected the birth of a nation, Federal was popular in the United States from 1790 until 1820. Various furniture designs such as Hepplewhite and Sheraton were adorned with eagles and other patriotic symbols.

SHAKER. Simple and functional (like the religious sect that created it), this furniture was designed and made in the United States from 1790 until around 1900. After 1860 it was sold to the secular market and is highly sought after today.

DIRECTOIRE. A link between Louis XVI and the Empire styles that followed, Directoire reflects Greek classicism that was influenced by the French Revolution. Made of mahogany in France between 1795 and 1799, chairs either have tops that curl back or backs that are concave. X supports are common. Chair arms often are a continuation of the cylindrical, tapering front legs. Designs of symbols considered patriotic to the Revolution were done in bas-relief.

SHERATON. This English style that closely resembles Hepplewhite, was popular from 1795 until 1810. Delicate and slender with fewer curves than Hepplewhite, it reflects the influence of Classic and Directoire styles. Turned legs are usually reeded or fluted and tapered to small squared feet, chair backs generally, but not always, are rectangular. Combinations of various woods were used, but mahogany was the most prevalent. Inlays and veneers were common. Ornaments used included urns, sunbursts, swags, and wheat ears. Striped fabrics were usually the choice for upholstery.

REGENCY. Made from 1795 until 1830, this English style is infamous for its uncomfortable chairs. Lines are straight, curves low, appearance is graceful. In place of carving, brass dolphins, swans, scrolls, and other ornaments were used. (Note: The French Regence spelling ends with an "e".)

DUNCAN PHYFE. This design was produced by America's most famous cabinetmaker, who made fine furniture from 1795 to 1847. His influence was greatest between 1800 and 1820. Phyfe refined the popular styles of his day: Directoire, Sheraton, and Empire. He was an excellent craftsman and all his furniture pieces were simple, yet graceful and elegant.

EMPIRE, FRENCH. A style of massive, heavy furniture made in France from 1805 to 1815. Lines, for the most part, are straight with lots of ornamentation. Its large, flat, plain surfaces were often adorned with marble. By today's standards, it's overdone.

EMPIRE, AMERICAN. The same massive furniture as French Empire, made in the United States between 1815 and 1840.

VICTORIAN. Furniture made in England and the United States during the reign of Queen Victoria—1837-1901. There are two styles: the more popular has large pieces with lots of decorative carvings and ornate gingerbread. The smaller, less desirable, style has less decoration.

EASTLAKE. English architect Charles Lock Eastlake expounded a return to simple, sturdy furniture—thus he was a harbinger of the

Arts and Crafts movement (see below). However, furniture manufacturers often corrupted Eastlake's first principle of "honest workmanship" with machine-made gingerbread tack-on moldings. This late Victorian style reflects Gothic and Japanese designs and was popular between 1868 and 1880.

COTTAGE. Inexpensive furniture made in this country between 1860 and the early 1920s, this furniture was mass-produced of pine. It has simple lines and is painted and often stenciled.

ANGLO-JAPANESE. This Oriental-looking furniture was made in the United States from 1880 until 1910. It is asymmetrical with turned legs and moldings that resemble bamboo. Decorations are of Oriental motifs.

ARTS AND CRAFTS. The antithesis of ornate Victorian furniture, this rectangular style is solid, simple, and hand-crafted—usually of oak—with solid joinery. Exposed slats were part of the design. The medieval and Japanese influences are unmistakable. Arts and Crafts furnishings were popular in England, Europe, and America from 1890 to 1920.

COLONIAL REVIVAL. From 1890 to 1925, American Colonial style furniture was again popular. Many of the reproductions produced at that time were inferior, and failed to hold true to the original lines and quality. However, there were several furniture makers who did follow the earlier style closely and their pieces are of quality.

ART NOUVEAU. Fanciful swirls and flowing lines, depicting flowers and other natural objects, mark this style. Introduced in 1895 in France and popular until 1910, very little of this style furniture was produced in the United States. The French were quite taken with it, embracing the style in buildings as well as furniture. On the other hand, Art Nouveau jewelry and other accessories were, and are again, popular in this country.

MISSION. A spin-off of the Arts and Crafts movement, this style furniture was manufactured in the United States from about 1900 to 1915. Plain, with straight and simple lines, chairs have vertical slat backs, and upholstered piece are done in leather. Machine-made of oak, the construction is of high quality and very durable. Gustav Stickley, American furniture maker, is credited with originating the Mission style. Pieces bearing his or his brothers' labels are in demand.

ART DECO/ART MODERNE. Speed, streamline, futuristic, mechanization, modern, geometric, abstract, all describe the spirit of this design. Tubular steel, chrome, glass, cane, wire, Bakelite (early plastic), lacquer, paint, veneered woods, and man-made fabrics were the materials used for the first time or in new ways to reflect a break from the past—in particular, Art Nouveau. Straight, abrupt lines are common, but so are functional curves. Often the material, such as tubular steel, dictates the shape. Popular from 1910 to 1940 in France and the United States.

DEPRESSION. A blanket name that covers copies of earlier period styles produced in the United States between 1920 and 1942, the term covers the decade prior to the actual economic depression. This furniture, manufactured for the masses, was inexpensive. Although the quality is not fine, and few of the pieces are authentic replicas, it's solid and superior to much of the low-to- medium-priced furniture produced today.

CONTEMPORARY MODERN. This covers a multitude of designs that continue in the tradition of Art Deco/Art Moderne. Although modern means contemporary, and all the styles of the past were at one time contemporary and thus modern, the term as it is currently used applies to the Art Deco style and later. These are styles that reflect Twentieth Century (and Twenty first Century) technology and methods of production. Danish and Scandinavian Modern are examples. Laminated wood and plastic, molded into sculptured tables and chairs, demonstrate modern furniture design's break with traditional furniture construction.

FURNITURE CONSTRUCTION

All furniture was made entirely by hand prior to the early 19th Century. Wood, natural fabrics, metal hinges and locks, and often ivory, horn, shells, and metal for ornamental decorations, went into crafting these pieces. In the early 1800s, water- and steam-powered machines—to cut, shape, and stamp decorations that were formerly hand carved—were introduced. Assembling and finishing were still done by hand, but the mechanical aids made it possible to produce furniture faster, more uniformly, and at a much lower price than was possible by the old method. The result was that households of modest financial means could afford to buy new quality furniture.

Most furniture made today is cut and shaped by machine. The lower-grade pieces are assembled and finished by machine or on a conveyer belt with powered hand tools. The surfaces are painted or veneered over cheaper woods or fabricated boards. Thin wood or plastic-coated, photographed wood grains comprise the veneers. Higher-priced furniture is made from better grades of wood, and the assembly and finishing are done by hand. The general rule of thumb is: the more expensive a piece, the more hand detailing there is. Materials used are: wood; manufactured boards such as plywood, particle and wafer board; steel, aluminum and other metals; plastic; (recently) concrete; and natural and synthetic fabrics.

They say you can't judge a book by its cover. It's also true that you can't always tell the construction of a furniture piece from it's outer appearance. The strength of a piece depends on solid, durable, structural joints—that's where two pieces of the frame are connected together and, in most cases, the joints are hidden from view. You can often turn the piece over and/or pull out drawers to find some of the joints. Nevertheless, joinery done with the simple mortise and tenon or dowels can be difficult to identify. Their presence may be deduced when other forms of attachment, such as screws or bolts, are not apparent in a piece that shows strength and good detailing. (More on this subject later.)

MORTISE-AND-TENON. For thousands of years the basic joint has been the mortise-and-tenon, and it's still the best. With this type of joint a wooden tongue or plug (the tenon) fits tightly in a matching slot in the receiving piece (the mortise). The tenon is formed by cutting away portions of the piece to be attached. The pieces fit precisely and are glued in place—as are all joints. Mortise-and-tenon joints are used in chair construction and to attach table legs, as well as other pieces.

DOVETAILS. A variation of the mortise-and-tenon joint, the dovetail joint is commonly used to attach the sides of drawers, chests, and other pieces with box-like structure, and also to join wide boards. Fingers are notched out of the joining edges so that they interlock—like fingertips. Through dovetails can be seen easily from inside or outside of the joint. Half dovetails, which go only part way through the board, can only be seen from the inside. This joint is often used to hold drawer fronts.

DOWELS. These are round wooden pins inserted into pre-drilled holes in the two surfaces to be joined. They are usually grooved to channel the glue and provide an escape for the surplus. A doweled joint is not as strong as the mortise and tenon and is an inferior substitute where the latter can be used. But the dowel is superior to nails and screws and is used in such places as the framework of upholstered pieces.

BISCUIT JOINTS. A recent innovation, the biscuit is a flat, elliptical-shaped insert made of beech-wood. Slots are cut in the two adjoining pieces and filled with a water-based glue. The biscuit is inserted—much like a dowel would be. However, the biscuit need not fit as precisely as a dowel because the glue swells the biscuit to a perfect fit. A double-biscuit joint uses two biscuits. It is claimed that these joints are as strong as mortise-and-tenon joints and are often used in, but not limited to, picture frames.

RABBET JOINTS. These joints are commonly used in place of the dovetail in drawers of low-cost furniture. The ends of the drawer's front are cut back half its thickness to accept the width of the sides. This forms L-shaped joints which are glued and nailed in place.

BUTT JOINTS. Also called L-joints, they are prevalent in low-priced furniture. Corner ends are simply overlapped and nailed or screwed in place. For the joints to have any lasting strength, they must be reinforced with glue blocks (wood blocks glued in place).

T-JOINTS. Basically the same as butt joints, but the pieces joined are not at a corner. These joints can be used to attach a brace or support-piece to a frame or secure it to a shelf. The pieces are locked into place with screws or nails and glue.

LAP JOINTS. These are the butt and T-joints strengthened by interlocking notches.

The backs of furniture pieces and the bottom of drawers should fit into grooves, not just be nailed to the bottom and/or back of the side pieces. Grooves not only add to the finished look, but add strength to the structure. This is particularly true on the bottom of drawers, which carry direct weight. Higher grades of furniture pieces have well-fitted plywood backs and drawers. Lower quality pieces are fitted with hardboard or similarly inexpensive materials. In the case of drawers, glue blocks should give additional support along the edges of the bottom—a minimum of two in front, the back, and the two sides.

Most joints should be reinforced by wood blocks glued in place. In quality furniture this is the rule. It may appear to be a case of belt and suspenders, but the added support is really necessary where weight and/or frequent stress is common, such as in chairs, dressers, and tables. Wood tables should have triangular corner braces and glue blocks spaced around the inner edges to secure the top.

Screws, brackets, braces, and other hardware are used to fasten, support, and strengthen joints, tops, and shelves. When this hardware is used in conjunction with mortise-and-tenon joints, it is a plus, but used alone it indicates inferior workmanship. However, in the case of furniture made with particleboard, such as TV stands and computer desks that must often be assembled by the buyer, hardware is necessary. Particleboard will not hold mortise-and-tenon joints. Although very strong, this manufactured material crumbles easily and requires biscuits and/or hardware to join.

Pre-Cut Furniture Construction

Furniture that comes in a flat carton and must be assembled by the buyer is relatively inexpensive. TV stands, computer desks, file cabinets, chests, bookcases, and more, are sold in knockdown versions. Although pre-cut, solid-wood pieces (including antique reproductions) can be purchased, most of this type of furniture is made of particleboard with plastic-coated paper surfaces. Some photographed wood grains look authentic, but most stand out like a costume wig. Thanks to the capabilities of modern machines to cut the various components with precise accuracy, the pieces can be put together with a few screws and a little glue.

Members of our family have bought and assembled various knockdown furniture units and have been satisfied with the results.

The consensus was if a problem in assembling occurred, it was due to faulty or muddled instructions not in the materials. None of the participants in our diminutive poll suggested the pieces were on par with fine furniture, but they were satisfied with their durability (normal wear) and functionality.

We picked up a used computer desk—well, more like a narrow table—at a garage sale five or six years ago. It's made of particleboard with an obvious imitation wood-grain finish and is no beauty, but it fits just right in a nook and continues to be functional. Perhaps the best part of buying this type of furniture on the secondary market is that someone else has had the doubtful fun of assembling it. We paid $4.00 for this stand and later found a similar one on sale in a discount store for $29.95 plus tax—disassembled. Used (assembled) knock-down furniture is readily available, and if the joinery is solid, offers functional storage and utility pieces for rock-bottom prices.

Metal Furniture Construction

The construction of metal chairs and tables is usually obvious to the eye. Joints are welded, brazed, soldered, or bolted. Pieces made of, or covered with, sheet metal (such as cabinets) require framing of wood or metal.

Upholstered Furniture Construction

There have been books—whole series— written about the secret life of upholstered furniture, and here we are attempting to cover this cryptic topic in only a few paragraphs. But we hope to hit a useful compromise between: "Everything there is to know about upholstery," and "Upholstery is fabric covering a frame."

Sometime before the written word appeared, our ancestors tired of dragging logs and large stones into their dens to sit on and invented the stool. A little later a bench was crudely fashioned, perhaps by a romantic, to accommodate two people. Once set in motion, technology is uncontrollable in its quest for the new and improved. So it's no surprise that within a millennium or two, our early relatives sat down on stools that had backs attached to them. This innovation allowed one to lean back in relative comfort, without the necessity of a wall. Never satisfied, somebody placed a fur skin on the wood seat and upholstery was born. The next tech leap was to stretch leather or woven textiles over a ridged framework. Early examples of this basic chair were discovered in ancient Egyptian tombs, and it is still much in use today in folding models such as campaign, boat, and director's chairs.

In Europe during the Middle Ages, loose cushions filled with down, feathers, wool, horsehair, and other materials were placed over stretched hide. In place of hide, cording was also used. It consisted of rope stringers running the length and width of the frame, providing more spring than leather.

During the 16th Century, upholstery was introduced when chairs and settees were covered with fabric—for looks, not comfort. Later, padding was added to better fit the fabric, extend its wear, and increase comfort. Then in the 1700s, along with the Industrial Age that so greatly altered life, springs were introduced and modern upholstery was born.

Traditional upholstered furniture pieces start with a solid, hardwood frame. If coil springs are used, they are attached to webbing, which is tacked to the backs and seats. The springs are anchored down to the webbing and frame with heavy twine. Four-way hand-tied springs are held in place with four knots equally spaced on each spring. Eight-way, hand-tied springs are, of course, better and considered the hallmark for construction. Listen for this term at auctions, and ask the sellers in other markets if the piece in question is eight-way hand tied. Under the webbing, there's a finely woven dust cover. Over the springs are layers of burlap, padding, muslin, and glazed cotton, topped with a decorative fabric.

Zigzag springs may be used in place of webbing and coil springs. These springs stretch flat across the frame. Various patented spring systems using zigzag or similar types of springs are used in some contemporary construction, all claiming to be as good as the eight-way, hand-tied coil spring. We prefer the latter.

In pieces that lack coil springs, foam padding is fitted directly over the webbing or solid wood backs and seats. When you're attending an auction, ask one of the auction staff what he or she knows about the construction of any piece in which you're interested. Some of these people are extremely knowledgeable.

FURNITURE FABRICS AND UPHOLSTERY

Your won't have fabric choices to make when you're choosing a used upholstered piece, unless you plan to recover it. But certain fabric characteristics, as well as color and design, should influence your furniture pick. The look, feel, color fastness, soil resistance, and durability of upholstery materials differ—often greatly. Some fade easily and should not be subjected to direct sunlight. Some absorb dirt more readily than others and are poor choices for heavy wear.

You'll find natural (organic as opposed to synthetic) materials on most pieces made before the late 1940s, if they still have their original upholstery. Rayon, the first synthetic fabric, was invented in 1884 by the Frenchman Hilsire de Chardonnet. He treated

wood pulp with solvents, then spun the resultant liquid into fibers. DuPont introduced Nylon in 1938. It was the first commercially successful man-made fabric completely synthesized from chemicals. Since that time, scores of synthetic fibers have been developed. Today, fabrics of blended natural and synthetic yarns are used more than any single-content fabric. While most man-made fibers used in upholstering are woven into fabrics, a second group are used to coat fabrics. Vinyl or rubber is applied to fabric backing to create leatherette or similar materials. Designs, grains, and textures are embossed to give the look of natural materials.

If the manufacture's tag is still attached—usually on the underside or under the cushions—it will tell the fabric makeup. If the tag has been removed and/or the piece recovered, identifying the fabric can be difficult, particularly if it's synthetic, and even more so when materials are blended.

Below are the most common fibers and their characteristics used in upholstery coverings:

Synthetic Fabrics

ACETATE. Lustrous look and luxurious feel. Accepts brilliant dyes as well as subtle color shades. Resists pilling and drapes well. Moderately priced. Poor resistance to wear and sunlight. Good qualities enhanced when blended with stronger fibers.

ACRYLIC. Wool-like feel. Takes bright colors and cleans well. Holds shape and pleats. Good resistance to fading, medium resistance to wear and pilling. Excellent in velvet and plush fabrics. Orlon is a trademarked acrylic fiber.

NYLON. Strong, very durable and cleans well. Down side: pills, fades, and soils easier than many other synthetic yarns.

RAYON. Excellent in strength, color fastness, stability, and resistance to pilling. Medium resistance to wear, abrasion, and sunlight. Blends well with other fibers.

OLEFIN. Very strong and durable. Resistant to abrasions, soil and fading. Sensitive to heat. Herculon is a trademarked olefin fiber.

POLYESTER. Similar to cotton in appearance and physical characteristics. Holds color and cleans well. Medium resistance to sunlight and wear. Dacron is a trademarked polyester fiber.

VINYL. Excellent soil resistance and easy to clean. Subject to abrasion and sunlight. Requires fabric backing for upholstery. Often used as an inexpensive substitute for leather.

Natural Fabrics

COTTON. Strong, durable, and soft to the touch. Little pilling. Not as color-fast as most synthetics. Only fair at resisting sunlight. Soils easily.

FLAX. Spun into linen. Has appearance much like cotton. Resists sunlight and soil better, is stronger, and more lustrous than cotton. New processes have reduced disposition for wrinkling.

LEATHER. Wonderful textures, durable, easily cleaned, and can be dyed any color. After tanning can be buffed with abrasives to produce suede; waxed, shellacked, or treated with pigments and resins for a smooth finish; or covered with urethane lacquer for a glossy patent finish.

SILK. Strongest of the natural fibers. Light, retains warmth, remains cool in hot weather, can absorb up to 30 percent of its weight in moisture without feeling clammy. Fire-resistant, (only burns while a flame is applied to it). Made into velvet, damask, and brocade materials. Often blended with other fabrics when used for upholstery.

WOOL. Has an agreeable feel, wears well, and holds color adequately. As with most other fibers, it's usually blended with other yarns.

Padding and Cushions

NATURAL. Until synthetic fibers were introduced to furniture manufacturing, upholstered pieces were padded with natural materials. The best material for this purpose was long, curled horsehair. Second quality consisted of Spanish moss (a tropical plant), low grades of cattle hair, or a mixture of hair and moss. The poorest quality padding was made of palm-leaf or cocoa fiber, sisal, flax or excelsior.

Cushions of the best grade were filled with goose down and feathers. Second best was soft duck, chicken and turkey feathers. Next came padded springs (after the 17th Century). Inferior pieces were padded with kapok, cotton, cotton linters (short fibers left on the cottonseed after the first ginning), or a mixture of these fibers.

SYNTHETIC. Following World War II, the use of synthetic fibers by furniture manufacturers rapidly increased to the point where, by 1960, pure natural fibers were seldom, if ever, used for padding and rarely used to fill cushions. Urethane foam and sponge rubber have become the standard padding materials. Chair and sofa cushions are now filled with polyester and other synthetic fiber fills or slabs of foam.

INSPECT BEFORE YOU BUY

Before you start shopping for used furniture, we suggest you read the chapter on *Repairing and Cleaning.* This will allow you to appraise any damage and/or imperfections in a piece so you can decide whether or not you can do what is necessary to restore it. Also, be aware that many, if not most, of the fine antique furniture pieces that sell for thousands of dollars at auction or grace the castles and manor houses of England and Europe are scarred. They have been lived with and on—some of them for hundreds of years—and show it.

Once you've selected a potential furniture buy, inspect it carefully. Slow down to a stop and just look. Start with the surface.

The wonderful and sturdy frame on this chair makes it well worth fixing up.
Not a difficult task for most amateurs.

Run your hand over the entire unit and feel for ripples, indentions, protrusions, and roughness. Look for areas that have been patched with wood or filler. Is there a smooth finish, is it uniform or faded in spots? Are there nicks, chips, scratches, worn spots, holes from nails and screws, or other blemishes? If a surface is veneered, is it damaged or loose? Do the top, sides, front panels, doors, or drawers show warping? Are the corners damaged? Is the back well fitted? Is it made of solid wood, plywood, or pressed board?

Move on to its construction. Is it sturdy, or does it wobble when you push on it? Check the joinery. Is the frame solidly braced? Do the drawers move in and out freely? Are there center guides? Are the drawers well constructed? Turn a drawer upside down and press on the bottom. Will it hold your weight? Tables that open to accept an expansion leaf should open and close with reasonable ease. If there is a leaf, check that it matches the table and properly aligns for an even fit. Is any hardware missing, such as handles, latches, and hinges? Are they attached securely and in good condition? Check chairs with fabric-covered seats, such as those used in dining rooms, for stains and heavy wear. Can the seat be removed easily so you can replace the fabric? Hutches and other tall units usually come apart in two sections for ease of moving. Do the sections firmly fit together, and are the sections original—or are they a marriage of units from different cabinets? Unless you expect an authentic antique, a furniture piece that has been created from two different sources is not necessarily bad if the parts harmonize and look pleasing to you, and you should be able to get it at a good price.

Metal furniture construction and condition are pretty obvious unless the piece is covered with fabric or other material. If it's a cabinet or chest, look inside to check the inner structure. In any case, lean on it to see if it wobbles. Check to see if rust has been covered over with paint, in which case the damaged area will be rough.

Upholstered furniture is more difficult to appraise than other furniture because most of the construction is concealed. However, you can often view the frame by tilting the piece forward and looking through the bottom dust cover. The cover may be thin enough to see through or have tears or other worn spots that allow you to peek inside. (We have found that a flashlight beam often will penetrate the cover and illuminate the inner structure.) Hopefully you can see if there are coil springs and how they're secured, or what other method of support is used. When you sit on a sofa or chair, lean your body against the back and feel its support. Is it lumpy, too hard, too soft, or just right? Assess the seat. How do the cushions feel? Do the cushions roll up at the corners from your weight? If they do, they're made of inferior foam material. Under the cushion(s), on the bottom of the piece, or in some other obscure place, a label should be stitched or glued to the cover giving the name of the manufacturer. Most major manufacturers have a reputation for the grade of furniture they produce. Because of this, the label suggests the quality of the original construction.

If the upholstery fabric is worn, consider the cost of slipcovers. We've mentioned slipcovers earlier, but they bear mentioning again.

Ask any questions you may have of the seller, but weigh the answers very carefully. The reply may be gospel, or it may be total fabrication. But the truth or fiction of a table being in the seller's family for five generations won't alter its rickety state, although it may be a good story to tell your friends. Condition should speak louder than anecdotes.

What's considered secondhand today will be antique tomorrow. The gently used items you select for your home will achieve this status in less time than anything you purchase new—and you'll put out far less money.

CHAPTER FOUR

Outfitting the Kitchen and Dining Room

WE'VE LUMPED these two rooms together because they both deal with food—either preparing it or enjoying it—and many of the items, such as dishes, may be used in either place. However, you don't need nearly the number of articles for a dining room as you do for an efficient kitchen.

In most states, a house that's sold or rented must have a working stove. So you've got a leg up on furnishing your kitchen. That's the good news. The bad news is that in order to have a well-functioning kitchen, you need a whole lot of gadgets— silverware, knives, a can opener, a corkscrew, a skillet (at least one), a minimum of three saucepans of graduated sizes, a pie plate, a cake pan, a jelly roll pan, a pizza pan, wooden spoons, metal spoons, slotted spoons, salt and pepper shakers, measuring cups, pot holders, and so forth. In addition you need (or at least will probably want) numerous small appliances such as a toaster or toaster oven, a microwave, an electric beater, a crockpot, an electric can opener, a bread machine,

A wall of intriguing kitchen utensils for sale in a coop offers useful as well as decoravtive items.

and that wonder of kitchen wonders a food processor. And don't forget the kitchen clock, and the curtains (if you're lucky enough to have a kitchen window or windows). Dish towels, a paper-towel rack, a dishtowel rack—we could go on and on.

GENTLY USED ESSENTIALS

The kitchen is, by far, the room that requires the most gadgets and tools. It's a work room, and you need whatever it takes to do the work. While many kitchen items aren't earth shatteringly expensive, taken together they add up to a good sum of money. If you need a refrigerator, you're talking big bucks. And, oh, you can do so much better on the secondary market. This is the room for which it is easiest to plan a color scheme. You may have to invest in a few cans of paint or rolls of wallpaper, but even these items are occasionally available pre-owned and unused.

At many auctions or tag sales held at homes, you'll find all of the spices, herbs, and extracts in one box lot; the cleaning supplies, dish detergents, sponges and so forth in another. The pots and pans all probably will be thrown into a large box and sold as a lot. The same applies to the loose stainless steel and sometimes silver-plate flatware that's been taken out of kitchen or dining room drawers. Often that same flatware put into a silver chest and offered for sale will bring several times as much money as it will loose. Presentation is a large part of the second-hand game, and that silver chest will add the note of elegance that makes people reach for their wallets especially if what's in it is silver plate. Although auctioneers know the silver chest will help, they seldom make the effort to provide one for silver plate or stainless steel because they're considered "everyday stuff." These types of sales are like hitting the jackpot for anyone who's outfitting a kitchen. Many garage sales also yield a plethora of the type of equipment you need to set up a kitchen.

A lovely mahogany table decorated with a collection of glass swans makes this
sunny dining room inviting.

Auction bidding, by design, goes fast so that the bidder doesn't have a chance to reason things out between bids. One legitimate, but confusing, method used by auctioneers is to put up an item in which there are a number of pieces—for instance two dozen glasses—and sell them by the piece, high bidder takes all. When you're caught up in the frenzy of bidding, it's easy to lose sight of the fact that while $5 doesn't seem like much to pay for one glass, when you multiply it by twenty four, you'll be putting out $120 for the set.

An auctioneer may have three sets of dishes of very unequal value to sell. In order to get the best price, all three sets of dishes can be put up at once with "choice" going to the high bidder. If you don't know anything about dinnerware, don't get into this one. Unless the high bidder is knowledgeable, he or she is just as likely to select the inferior set over the superior ones. The second highest bidder, who was probably after the best set, will then have choice of the two left or the bidding on the two will start again. In other words, the high bidder was driven to accelerate his bids by the competition. Bidding on someone else's knowledge is never more misguided than in situations like this.

Occasionally, very handsome sets of glasses numbering as many as one hundred or more pieces are offered. They're met with little enthusiasm. After all, who needs a hundred or more matched glasses? (Except maybe a caterer!) Our solution is to purchase them if the price is right, take out what we want for ourselves, divide the rest up into sets of eight or twelve, and use them as gifts. We've even bought Waterford Crystal this way.

Baskets in all shapes and sizes abound. Some are lovely and old, others are of a more recent vintage. They have many uses in a kitchen or dining room. If the tops of your cabinets don't reach the ceiling, you have a perfect place for a decorative row of baskets. An arrangement of short-stemmed flowers in a bowl of water set in a basket is pleasing on a dining room or kitchen table. A medium-sized basket filled with fresh or waxed fruits works well on a kitchen counter, in the center of a table, or on a dining room sideboard. We use a basket for a napkin holder in our kitchen. Most older baskets are smooth to the touch because the roughness has worn off from years of handling. In most types of baskets, the closer the weave, the better the basket.

Among the many linens you'll encounter at the various types of sales are napkins and tablecloths with stains, cigarette burns, and worn spots. You can buy boxes of these for almost nothing. In some cases, an auctioneer can't even get a bid without combining merchandise like this with good stuff in one lot. At one auction we got a fairly large box of damaged napkins and a couple of badly worn tablecloths for twenty-five cents! In the lot there was a dozen pink napkins—four of them were in tatters and we threw them out immediately. The others had small, stubborn stains or cigarette holes. The answer was to cover the spots with little sew-ons from the five and dime. These particular ones were in the form of roses. They weren't all sewn onto the same area of each napkin, but they

A truly spectacular buy! This Henredon ding room set with six chairs and two extension leaves was almost new when we got it for $200 at auction. The Mikasa dishes, a service for twelve, cost us $80.

made the napkins more interesting than they would have been if they'd been perfect. We did the same thing to one of the table-cloths and, although it was white and the napkins pink, the sew-ons made them blend together. This same method can be used on other linens as well.

Keeping a kitchen neat can be a frustrating job. People tend to use the counter as a catchall. We solved this problem with an old bicycle basket that we bought at a garage sale and attached just inside the kitchen door. Lined with material, it holds keys, books, maps, or whatever junk used to end up spread all over the kitchen.

Kitchen Collectibles

You'll find dishes, pots and pans by the boxful, linens, gadgets, everything (and we do mean everything) you need to furnish a kitchen or dining room in the markets of recycled goods. But in addition to the essentials, you want these rooms to have as much pizzazz as the rest of your home.

If you want a days-gone-by atmosphere, auctions and flea markets are your best bets. Collectors are active buyers of old kitchen wares, but if you don't want to pay top dollar, you'll find that there are usually items that slip through the cracks at any auction. As far as flea markets are concerned, the early bird gets the collectible.

There are three main categories of kitchen collectibles:

☛ The wonderful hand-made articles that were used for what is called "hearth cooking" (preparing meals over an open fireplace). These usually one-of-a-kind items—such as old food mills, chopping knives, or long-handled skimmers—were in use from the 1600s until the early 1800s. Some of them can still be used in today's modern kitchen, but the great preponderance serve as decorative reminders of our ancestors. Examples from this category are the most highly prized and quite expensive.

☞ As coal and wood stoves became common in American kitchens around the mid 1800s, manufacturers began mass producing utensils to replace the hand-made ones of earlier days. These easier-to-come-by, far-less-expensive articles make wonderful kitchen displays, and many people use them to prepare and serve food.

☞ In the 1920s, the gas stove was hailed as a boon to housewives everywhere—no more scrubbing soot off the kitchen walls. Electricity challenged gas in the cooking arena a few years later, and they've been duking it out ever since. Of course, the advent of these two types of stoves resulted in a rush by manufacturers to make implements suited to use with them. It was at this time that small electric appliances came on the scene. Although these older, mass-produced items have met with indifference in the past, they're starting to appeal to a certain segment of collectors. Electric waffle irons, electric toasters, and electric irons are gaining a small following but are still extremely reasonable, and some are quite handsome.

The Rustic Look

If you're going for a rustic look in your kitchen, a wall of small, early hand utensils will help establish the tone you're after. A nutmeg grater, nutcracker, and a cabbage cutter would be interesting. Our favorite graters are the tiny nutmeg graters that were carried by gentlemen in the 1800s so they could grate nutmeg into their libations when they were away from home. These graters have innovative designs and any one of them would make a fanciful and useful addition to a group of kitchen collectibles. Or try tying some cookie cutters with six to eight-inches of rope or decorative string between each one. Hang the rope from a hook in the ceiling. A mortar and pestle adds interest to a shelf or kitchen counter.

You might want a mechanical apple parer. The first one was invented by Moses Coates in 1803. Many modifications have been made to the various models that have been marketed since that time. This mechanical device made it possible to remove the peel of an apple in one piece by just turning a handle. It still beats a paring knife! Cherry pitters, raisin seeders, meat grinders, fruit presses, food mills—inventive minds have continued to add work-saving devices for use in the kitchen.

Many early 20th century kitchen items, such as ice cream scoops, were tin or nickel plated. Most of this plating has become worn with the years of use, and this does detract from the value. For instance, a worn nickel-plated ice cream scoop has lost some of its worth. However, if you take that scoop and wirebrush all of the nickel off it, leaving the metal beneath, you'll be removing its value along with the nickel. Unfortunately, this is just what some dealers have done. Watch for this when you're buying old nickel-plated items.

From the 1920s through the 1940s, red and green were popular kitchen colors. As a result, there were many wooden-handled bottle openers, mashers, can openers, mixing spoons, etc. of these colors. Those that have survived are very desirable to collectors. The degree of wear on the paint is an important factor, but we've seen these items in perfect condition sell for less than you'd pay for their new, plastic counterparts.

Old wooden bowls, some of them hand-carved, are both useful and attractive—but a bit pricey. You can just as easily get a nest of colorful Pyrex bowls for next to nothing at an auction or garage sale.

Solving Mysteries

Some of the kitchen helpers that have been invented over the years are strange-looking. So strange-looking, in fact, that it's often difficult—if not impossible—to discern their intended use. While it's fun to own and display oddities, the fun is increased if you have an answer when someone asks you what they are. If you have a mystery item, look for a patent number. (You may also find a date). If you write to the U.S. Patent office giving them the number and explaining your dilemma, they will be able to tell you something about your acquisition, including its purpose.

GREAT GOODIES FOR THE KITCHEN

The following is an assessment of some additional items you might want to consider for your kitchen or dining room. It's by no means a complete list—it would take volumes to cover everything that's available. But we hope it will give you some ideas and start your creative juices flowing.

BOTTLES. Displayed in windows, where they catch the light of the sun's rays, bottles can really brighten up a room. The most collectible American-made bottles were hand-blown between 1810 and 1910. (After that machines took over the job.) Early bottles are usually green or blue, although there are some amber or brown examples. They generally have a great many bubbles and other imperfections. This doesn't detract from their value.

Bottles were made in many shapes including animals, buildings, guns and canons, and people. They were used for medicines, whiskey, tonic, and a host of other things. Figural bottles are hot items, especially if they're embossed with the likeness of a known person, such as a president or other political figure. They're so hot, in fact, that they've been widely reproduced. Barber shop bottles, that once contained the hair dressings and after shave lotions used on gentlemen patrons, are highly collectible and handy for oil and vinegar and other kitchen liquids.

Mineral water from various spas was bottled with the name of the particular spa embossed on the bottle. Most of them are green, a few are amber, and the most prized come from old spas that have been defunct for many years.

Age is an important factor in the value of a bottle. A raised circle of glass on the bottom of a bottle came from a glob of glass that was used to hold the bottle in place at the end of a rod, called a pontil, while the glass blower shaped the neck after which the pontil and the glass glob were broken off, leaving the circle of glass. This dates a bottle to 1850 or before. From 1850 to about 1860, the pontil was heated and used to melt the glass on the bottom of the bottle just enough to attach it firmly to the pontil. When the pontil was removed it left a black, red, or white circular mark. Bottles made after 1860 usually have smooth bottoms.

BOXES. There are so many types of boxes used for so many different things. Take an old recipe box, for instance, full of some family's treasured favorites. This is a charming and useful addition to any kitchen. Salt boxes and match boxes were standard items in old kitchens and are frequent auction offerings. Watch out for crazing (networks of fine cracks through the finish) on old salt boxes and be aware that salt boxes have been reproduced. Ice boxes were a staple in every home. The "better homes" had fancier, bigger renditions of this necessity. They were pretty much discarded after refrigerators became available even to lower-income homemakers. Sometime in the 1970s, it became fashionable to resurrect old oak ice boxes, refinish them, and use them for everything from liquor cabinets to replacements for bureaus in bedrooms. The craze has died down to some extent, but ice boxes still look pretty cool in a kitchen. At one time, we had one in which we stored napkins, plastic wrap, paper towels, and other paper products. They also make good bread boxes. Ice boxes have been reproduced. We've yet to see a good, authentic reproduction, however.

BREAD MACHINES. The modern electric bread machines available in stores today are marvels at cutting down the work of bread making. But they're a novelty, and kitchen novelties get used for awhile and then are abandoned and start appearing on the secondary markets. As of this writing, it's too soon for this to happen with these machines. However, old breadmakers, the bread machines of the past, appear on the market from time to time. Most are made of tin, iron, or aluminum, or a combination of these metals, and have instructions for their use printed right on the lid—no booklets to lose. Landers, Frary, and Clark of New Britain, Connecticut seems to have been the chief manufacturer of these machines which look like a pail with a lid from which protrudes a handle. After mixing the ingredients well with the handle, the dough was allowed to rise in the pail. They're not as easy to use as the electric machine but not as expensive either—about a third the cost—and still much easier than doing it by hand.

BUTTER CHURNS. Of course, the idea of these churns was to churn cream until it separated and formed beads of butter. The taste of freshly churned, unsalted butter was far superior to what the supermarkets have to offer. But the churning was work. Today you can still find some tall, wooden churns with what looks like a broom stick coming out the top. These originally were painted, and if you're fortunate, you'll find one with the original paint in reasonable condition. Repainting greatly diminishes the value. This type of churn is attractive in the corner of a kitchen or breakfast nook.

A glass, hand-turned butter churn looks right at home on a kitchen counter, and there are electric churns of a later vintage. Try and get one that has good graphics on the front. Glass butter churns are the easiest to find a place for, and they're the least expensive of the churns. Most examples of butter churns are from the late 1800s through the early 1900s.

BUTTER MOLDS. Some butter molds were hand-made others were manufactured. Freshly churned butter was pressed into the mold, where it hardened into the shape of the mold.

Dairy farmers often sold their products, including butter, and in some areas each farmer had his own particular mold that identified butter from his farm. Some butter molds were made of wood—other, commercial ones, were from glass. The glass cow and swan designs have been widely reproduced.

BUTTER PRINTS. Used to decorate butter, we've seen these usually handcarved, wooden prints in sizes anywhere from about an inch to three or four inches. These prints were pressed into the tops of butter pats or cubes of butter, depending on the size. Some are rectangular, some round. Some have handles, others don't. A collection of the handleless variety, hung over a sink or stove, works well as a spot of decoration. You'll find the acorn (which was the most popular, probably because it was an easy one to carve) at most sales that offer any butter prints. More elaborate, more desirable examples were designed by some accomplished, though amateur, artisans. Many molds were also made by machine and are reproduced today. Serving decorated pats of butter adds a note of elegance to any dinner party.

CANDY CONTAINERS. The fun of collecting these little glass replicas of everything from lanterns to battleships is finding unusual shapes. Candy containers are being widely reproduced and bought up at exorbitant prices by the unwary. The original candy containers were produced in Jeanette, Pennsylvania from 1876, when little candies were sold in reproductions of the Liberty Bell and Independence Hall, until 1960 when the candy container business went belly up due to lack of interest. By this time, the many other shapes had been introduced. Although a few other companies made these small candy containers during their heydays, the lion's share of the manufacturing remained in Jeanette. Old examples with the original candy are quite difficult to find but with the label that sealed the container intact they're sometimes worth hundreds of dollars. Reproductions have been made for many years and are still in production. They usually have a slightly oily feeling to the glass. Friends of ours have a collection of candy containers on a shelving unit in their dining room. None of the containers is real old (a fact they knew when they purchased them at a flea market), but that doesn't stop people from admiring them and asking questions about the collection.

CARNIVAL GLASS. This inexpensive-expensive glass was made from 1905 until about 1929. We call it inexpensive-expensive because it was first made so that people with average or below average incomes could own glass that was supposedly comparable to Tiffany's Fravile with its iridescent finish. The makers of Carnival glass achieved a luster on their products by covering them with a sodium solution before firing the pieces. The amount of luster you'll find on a piece is directly related to how much sodium solution was applied. This glowing surface covered a multitude of imperfections in this inferior glass. Carnival glass was inexpensive then. But now the price has taken on a life of its own—pieces that sold originally for one or two dollars may be auctioned for $500, $1,000 or more. That's what we call appreciation.

Almost all Carnival glass was made by one of four companies—Millersburg Glass Company (which only was in business from 1909 until 1912), Northwood Glass Company, Fenton Art Glass Company, and Imperial Glass Company. Northwood marked some, but not all, of its pieces with an "N" in a circle. Imperial sometimes marked its pieces with an iron cross. The other companies wares were unmarked.

Carnival glass is being reproduced widely. Some examples are actual copies of older pieces, some come from the old molds, others are entirely new designs.

Unfortunately, much of this new glass is being sold as old, original Carnival glass. Newer pieces often have more iridescence than the older pieces on which the original surface has worn off a bit. We don't think old Carnival glass is worth anywhere near the prices it brings. But if you like the look of it, go for newer pieces that are being sold as new at a price that reflects not only their age but their quality. There are pretty canister sets, biscuit jars, bowls, and glasses that you can use to spruce up your kitchen or dining room.

CAST-IRON COOKWARE. Many people swear that cast-iron pots and pans are the only pans worth cooking with. These utensils were mass produced from about 1850 until 1940, when lighter cookware became popular. Griswold and Wagner are the two best known names and command the highest prices. A few Griswold skillets have brought as much as $1,000 at auction. However you'll find other, lesser known makes for as little as fifty cents at garage sales and for not much more at flea markets and auctions. These pans, in graduated sizes, are both decorative and useful. You can either hang them on a wall or store them in a glass-front cabinet where they can be displayed and admired. The most experienced cooks claim that cast iron pans never should be washed—just seasoned with oil and wiped out with a damp cloth after each use.

COFFEE GRINDERS. There's something about the aroma of freshly ground coffee that turns even the most austere kitchen into a friendly place. Both modern, plastic coffee grinders and well-used old ones are fairly plentiful. We much prefer the older varieties, and since buying specialty coffees and grinding one's own coffee beans has become fashionable, grinders appear in more and more decorating schemes. Some of the older examples have been painted, converted into lamps, or otherwise altered, rendering them almost worthless.

Some of the names to look for on old coffee grinders are Adams, Bronson-Walton, Daisy, Elgin National, Elma, Lane Brothers, Parker, Regal, Sun, and Swift. These often slip by for a pittance at garage sales, where the neophyte considers them just an old, outdated appliance.

COOKBOOKS. What could be a more natural addition to a kitchen than a shelf of cookbooks? However, we advise you to display your cookbooks on a shelf in a glass front cabinet to protect them from the inevitable grease and cooking odors that permeate a kitchen. The interest in cookbooks sparked around 1900 (although there had been several good "cookery books" before this) and peaked somewhere in the early 1980s. During these years there were cookbooks on every imaginable subject including general cookbooks, health-related cookbooks, time-saving cookbooks, gourmet cookbooks, celebrity cookbook—the list goes on. Most of them have found their way to the secondary markets.

Originally cookbooks were written by women who had developed recipes on their own. Many of these ladies cooked their favorite dish for a church supper only to find the creation so well received that the other ladies of the church asked for the recipe—the ultimate compliment! The pastors and ladies clubs of the churches saw the exchange of recipes as a way to add a little money to the church coffers, and they encouraged parishioners to submit recipes for inclusion in books and pamphlets. Some fine recipes came out of these efforts. And this type of collection is a fun addition to a kitchen of today.

Almost any appliance, large or small, that was introduced in the 20th century resulted in a number of cookbooks instructing people how to get the most out of the particular appliance or gadget. Some people collect only this form of cookbook.

Cookbook collectors don't necessarily make the recipes in their cookbooks; often they only use them for show. For instance, one might display a cookbook holder with a plastic shield that holds the book and reveals the open pages. There are some cookbooks with beautiful color illustrations that lend themselves to this treatment. Some cookbooks have mouth-wateringly delicious jacket illustrations and/or color photographs between the covers. These pictures are suitable for framing and hanging on a kitchen wall.

COOKIE CUTTERS. Old hand-made cookie cutters bring a good price at auction because they're one of a kind, usually fashioned by the man of the house or an itinerant worker. Old cutters made from scrap metal are generally at least one-inch deep and often as deep as two inches, while the more modern cutters have cutting strips of no more than one-half inch. The cutting strips of the older cutters were soldered to the top piece, usually in a sloppy manner, most aren't as perfect as the newer, mass produced varieties. For instance, a bird might have wings of unequal size or a rabbit's ears could be too large for the body. These defects just endear the cutters to today's collectors. Handles on old cookie cutters were made from the same material as the cutter, from a scrap of leather, or a piece of wood fashioned into a round knob. One collector we know made dough cookies with her unusual molds, lacquered the cookies, dressed them up with calico ribbons, and hung them on her kitchen wall. Other people take the easy route and display the cookie cutters.

COOKIE JARS. Almost every kitchen boasts a cookie jar, whether it's used for cookies or just for a display. Old cookie jars are highly desirable and a collector will pay a good price to fill out a collection. Sometime in the 1930s, manufacturers began making figural cookie jars instead of the plain, barrel-shaped type that had been offered previously. People loved the imaginative shapes and so the manufacturers created more designs, and they're still coming up with new and different cookie jars.

Some of the names to look for in cookie jars are Abington, American Bisque, Belmont, McCoy, California Originals, Hall, Hull, Mar-Crest, Napco, Pan American Art, Poppy Trail by Metlox, Red Wing, Robinson Ransbottom, Shawnee, Sierra Vista, Twin Winton, and Walt Disney. Some of the examples are newer, but at most auctions cookie jars, new or old, sell for way beyond their worth. At garage sales, however, you'll find them at extremely low prices. If you want an old jar, be aware that many styles have been reproduced.

CORKSCREWS. Ever since the seventeenth century, when people started putting corks in bottles, other people have been trying to get them out. As a cork gets wet, it swells, making the task of removing it daunting if you lack the proper equipment. Over the years, corkscrews in all shapes and sizes have been invented. Many of them were not up to the task for which they were created and have gone on to be oddities in the collecting field. Others work masterfully well. Old, figural corkscrews are particularly desirable. Owning just one can make opening a bottle of wine a more special event—a collection is a delightful conversation piece.

EGG BEATERS. In 1870 the rotary egg beater was patented. Housewives loved it—so much in fact that they pretty much abandoned using any of the other 140 egg beaters that had previously received patents. (In order to receive a patent, an object must be significantly different from any other object that's already been patented.) That gives you an idea of the diversity of methods used before rotary beaters, and there have been many variations of the rotary type since that breakthrough in 1870. Except for a few outstanding beaters, this is an inexpensive and "unbeatable" collectible. You may prefer to have just one to display and use in your kitchen or a set of different beaters hanging on a wall. Many old beaters are marked with a date and patent number.

GRANITEWARE. In the latter half of the 1800s, enamel coating was applied in various swirl or mottled patterns over plain metal coffee pots, kettles, molds, ladles, bowls, and pans that had been staples in kitchens. This enamel graniteware, alas, didn't live up to its name, and one good bang against a faucet or sink and the decorative coating chipped. Today graniteware is collected; but many, if not most, of the old pieces have at least a few dings.

While this does reduce the price, it doesn't seem to discourage the collector. Dark blue and white, green and white, brown and white, and red and white are considered very desirable. While Graniteware is impractical to cook with (unless you're extremely careful and not accident prone), it does look nice on a hanging pot rack or neatly placed on a shelf. Graniteware has been widely reproduced, and we're suspicious of any piece that doesn't have any signs of wear.

ICE CREAM MOLDS. Although the type of gracious dining that included such things as ice cream served in various shapes met its demise with the advent of working women and convenience foods, some of the accoutrements of these by-gone niceties add interest to a home. Ice cream molds are included in this category. Most ice cream molds are made of tin and range from geometric shapes to figures of animals, birds, and patriotic subjects. Some are small and make individual servings—others were made to hold enough to serve several people. The animal and bird figures are the most sought after. Look for examples with well defined details in the designs.

KNIVES. Every efficient kitchen needs at least a few good knives. One for paring, one for carving, one for slicing bread, one for boning chicken—the list goes on. New knives, the kind that hold an edge and really get the job done, can take a good chunk out of a week's pay. When you're searching the secondhand markets for cutlery look for the names Case, Queen, Remington, and Western States.

Sterling carving sets are plentiful, too. But the word sterling is usually misleading. The only thing that's sterling is the covering over a weight that's in the handle. Neither the blade nor the core of the handle are sterling. Thus it's impossible to determine how much sterling, by weight, is in either the carving knife or the fork that accompanies it. These sets are handsome and if you carve at the table when you have guests (a sort of old-fashioned concept) you may want one. Look both pieces over well for the denting that's common in weighted sterling pieces, and don't pay much.

LUNCH BOXES. There are four categories of lunch boxes: The first were actually square, metal tobacco boxes fashioned with a handle so they could be used as lunch boxes. These containers, made in the early 1900s, appeal to people who like old advertising graphics. The second, and least desirable, were plain colored, had a camel back top to accommodate a thermos, and were carried by workmen. The third category, oval tin boxes with dogs, cats, children at play—anything that would appeal to kids—was made by Decoware and Ohio Art from the 1930s until the 1950s. The fourth type of lunch box was born when Aladdin Industries marketed a metal box with the likeness of Hopalong Cassidy adorning it. Kids loved it. Adults loved it. This smashing success was the beginning of an industry that still thrives today, but most modern lunchboxes are made of plastic.

Condition and the presence of the original thermos, if there was one, are very important in this collectible. Newer lunch boxes, even plastic ones are sold for far more than they brought new. For example, a 1987 Yogi Bear's Treasure Hunt lists in price guides at $30. If you have a spot in your kitchen (or another place in your home) for collectibles of this type, but don't want to invest big money, travel the garage sales and buy more recent models. If they're in good condition, they should appreciate. Meanwhile, you can enjoy the graphics.

MASHERS. There are more forms of mashers, old and new, than there are things to mash. Our favorite type is called a "beetle." Most beetles were hand-made. A bettle has a long handle at one end and a wooden cube or knob at the other end and was used to mash vegetables. Examples carved from one continuous piece of wood, instead of with a handle that was attached to the business end, are more valuable. A beetle is a fine addition to any collection of old kitchen utensils.

MORTARS AND PESTLES. Mortars are small bowls in which pharmacists ground drugs into usable powders with a pestle, which is simply a solid rod used as a masher. The mortar and pestle match. The most common examples are made from wood, cast iron, stoneware, brass. Not only is a mortar and pestle a decorative addition to a kitchen, it's a useful one as well. We have an old brass set sitting on our kitchen counter that gets a workout grinding herbs and spices to just the right consistency. Auctions and coops are the best sources for a mortar and pestle, and although you'll find a wide range of prices, most of them are well within range of the average pocketbook.

NUTCRACKERS. Getting nutmeats out of their tough shells has always presented a challenge. The standard nutcracker of today with two metal rods hinged at the top is uninteresting at best and doesn't accomplish the job as well as the nutcrackers of old. Figural nutcrackers in shapes from alligators to squirrels—from cherubs to parrots—from dogs to donkeys—are delightful to display and to use. Most of the older nutcrackers you'll find on the secondary markets were made from the middle of the 1800s until well into the 20th century. They crack nuts in ingenious ways. For example, if you put a nut in the dog's mouth and pull its tail down, the animal's mouth will close, cracking the nut. We've seen a great many reproductions of old nutcrackers. Many dealers have them marked as new and sell them at a corresponding price.

PIE BIRDS. These vents to let the steam out of pies while they're baking have been around since the Victorian era. Hollow and open at the bottom with a small vent or opening at the top, the original pie bird was in the shape of a blackbird. But while the name has stayed the same, the designs have changed and now include elephants, people, buildings, and a host of other shapes. The old pie birds are fairly expensive but newer ones, which are bright and do the job, are plentiful and very inexpensive. To use a pie bird, you cut a hole the size of the bottom of the pie bird in the upper crust of a pie. Put the pie bird in the hole before you put the pie in the oven.

REFRIGERATOR DISHES. You have your choice of plastic refrigerator dishes at almost any estate sale where all of the household goods are sold along with the better things. We dislike plastic containers. They hold odors, they hold stains, and most of them warp. Our solution is to look for the older covered glass refrigerator dishes that are fairly plentiful. They're dishwasher safe, can be used in a freezer, and you can even cook in most of them. These little gems turn up at flea markets, garage sales, auctions, and at coops in great numbers.

ROLLING PINS. Whether you make your own pastry or opt for one of the several varieties of prerolled offerings from the supermarket, you'll probably want a rolling pin in your kitchen. The older ones that you'll find are mostly made of wood, although some were made of tin and filled with ball bearings or something else to give them weight. Wooden rolling pins date from the late 1800s until the present. In the 1920s glass rolling pins became popular. The idea was to fill the glass with ice water thus keeping the shortening in the pastry from getting soft while it was rolled out. It was a good idea.

Unless you want an unusual rolling pin, and there are many of them, this won't be a major kitchen expense.

STEINS. In order for a beer mug to qualify as a stein, it must have a hinged lid. Most steins were and are made in Germany—a few are American, but these are spurned by collectors. Early steins, those made at the beginning of the nineteenth century, aren't very attractive and there's little interest in them.

The most important names to look for in steins are Villeroy and Boch, Mettlach Merkelblach and Wick, Albert Jacob Thewalt, and Simon Peter Gerz. Between the late 1800s and early 1900s, a type of decoration called chromoliths were made by Villeroy and Boch in Mettlach, Germany. These designs have a three-dimensional look, although they're actually smooth. The closely guarded secret of achieving this was lost in a fire in the factory. Although efforts have been made to reconstruct this method, no one has ever been successful in creating a good duplicate. Cameo designs are also highly prized. Starting in the 1970s, duplications of old steins were marketed. These are stamped with the date and are easily recognized. The condition of a stein is paramount in determining its value.

If you want a collection of steins to display in your dining room or kitchen but don't want to pay the going prices, start with American steins. Some of them are quite attractive. Even Avon makes decorative steins that can be had for a few dollars.

DINNERWARE

Elegant dinnerware fit for royalty is waiting for you at auctions at a fraction of what it would cost you new. A short time ago, we purchased a twelve-place setting of Lenox china in the Blue Ridge pattern for $325. The set had everything, including serving pieces, bouillon cups and saucers, demi tasse cups and saucers, luncheon and dinner plates, and all the other pieces that go into an elaborate and complete set of fine china. Even on sale, a new set like this one would have cost thousands of dollars.

The range of quality and value of dinnerware is wide. At the top of the line, you'll find gold or silver trimmed porcelain—at the bottom, glass and plastic. The following definitions should help you understand what is being offered at a sale or auction:

BONE CHINA. A hard-paste porcelain containing up to 40 percent bone ash, bone china is translucent, delicate, and usually expensive.

CERAMIC. Clay items fired at high temperatures.

CHINA. Technically, china is high-quality porcelain or ceramic ware, but the term is commonly used as a synonym for dinnerware and is no guarantee of quality.

CRAZING. A network of fine cracks that develops in the glaze of low-fired pottery as a result of uneven shrinkage or age. Crazed dinnerware should be avoided.

EARTHWARE. Pottery that's at least 50 percent porous. It can be either glazed or unglazed.

GLASS-CERAMIC. Patented formulas that contain a mixture of glass and clay to enhance their strength and durability.

GLAZE. A thin, smooth, glassy coating applied to earthware and porcelain, leaving it impervious to liquids. It can be dull or glossy, translucent or opaque, clear or colored.

HARD-PASTE PORCELAIN. Porcelain that is composed mainly of kaolin, a fine white clay. It's hard and durable.

IRONSTONE. A fairly durable, hard, white, glazed pottery.

OPAQUE. Anything that completely blocks out the light.

PORCELAIN. A hard, very fine-grained, white ceramic ware that is translucent.

POTTERY. Clay ware fired at a low temperature.

SEMIPORCELAIN. Pottery with the tough glaze used on porcelain.

SOFT-PASTE PORCELAIN. A porcelain that contains a high percent of bone ash. It's easily chipped or broken.

STONE CHINA. An inexpensive, hard, white earthenware.

STONEWARE. A dense, hard-paste, non-porous pottery.

STRAW MARKS. Imperfections created in the mold, straw marks are caused by lint or other waste material that burns up but leaves a scar.

TRANSLUCENT. A substance through which light shows.

TRANSFER DESIGN. A decoration printed on, or applied to the ware as a decal. It can be either under or over glaze.

Getting Your Money's Worth

All porcelain and bone china are not equal. Even under the same manufacturer's name, there can be a range of grades. Less expensive china grades show below par workmanship and should sell at lower prices. Compared to the better china, they may be heavier, show imperfections in the glaze, and with a magnifying glass you'll usually find that the edges of the design aren't sharp. Although translucent, the quality of the material is inferior.

To determine whether a piece is porcelain or bone china, test it for translucency by holding a piece up to the light and touching your finger to the underside of the piece. You should easily see the shadowy form of your finger through the material.

When you look over a set of dinnerware, take the time to check for the following: cracks and chips; glued pieces; crazing; knife marks on plates; worn patterns, particularly around the edges of plates and bowls; straw marks and other surface imperfections; uneven color and glaze, including drip marks on the undersides of pieces. With a full set of dishes this is time consuming, but it's worth it. You may want an imperfect set, but you should know what you're getting and your bid should reflect the condition of the dinnerware.

You'll find that dinnerware that's considered collectible commands lofty prices well above it's intrinsic value.

DEPRESSION GLASS. This is an example of a glass that's taken off in popularity and now sells at ridiculously high prices, Depression glass was made just prior to and during the Great Depression into the 1940s, when production ceased. It was sold in five-and-dime stores, by mail order, and was given away as premiums at gas stations, theaters, and stores. The object of these premiums was to give out one piece at a time, keeping those interested in obtaining an entire set coming back until they had achieved their goal.

This inferior, molded glass was made in over 25 colors and approximately 100 designs. The royal lace pattern made by Hazel Atlas Glass Company is especially desirable to collectors. Many companies, including Federal Glass Company, Hocking Glass Company, Indiana Glass Company, and Jeanette Glass Company made Depression glass. There are zillions of reproductions, some better than the originals. Depression glass is out-of-sight at auctions, but occasionally a piece, or even an entire set, turns up at a garage sale where it's usually a spectacular buy.

PRESSED GLASS. Old pressed glass will dress up your table or look impressive displayed in a cabinet, and most of it won't cost you a fortune.

Machine-pressed glass, invented in the early 19th century, is plentiful in many forms from berry bowls to toothpick holders. There are two basic types of pressed glass: Lacy Glass, which has a background of stippled dots with designs on the unstippled areas, and Pattern Glass, which isn't stippled. The stippling in Lacy Glass was done to cover a multitude of bubbles and other flaws—a task it performs well.

There are some beautiful pressed glass pieces available. Pricing loosely follows certain guidelines: The larger a piece the more it will cost. A covered dish is worth more than an open dish. An old piece of pressed glass, even though it has more flaws than a newer one, is worth more money. Many pieces of old pressed glass were flashed with gold or gold decorations. Worn flashing seriously devalues a piece.

Much of the pressed glass was made in Europe, especially in France. These pieces are easy to identify because they are a good deal heavier than the American pieces. Heisey Glass, which was made in Ohio from 1896 until 1957, is highly collectible. Most examples are marked with an H in a diamond. (This mark isn't always easy to spot. You'll often find it tucked away in some obscure place.)

There's no reason why goblets, water glasses, or serving pieces need to match to be used together. In fact, we think a variety of patterns makes for a much more inviting table. And pressed glass looks lovely displayed on a dark background with light shining on it. It doesn't sparkle quite as much as good cut glass or crystal, but then it doesn't cost as much either.

There are many pressed glass pieces that get lost in the bottoms of box lots at auctions. We've bought them when they were so filthy we couldn't see the pattern. But a good soaking has brought them to life. Warning! Don't put old glass in a dishwasher.

STERLING SILVER FLATWARE. Neither the very best silver plate flatware nor the most expensive stainless steel will make your table reflect the glow of elegance like sterling silver will. But have you checked sterling prices in your local department store recently? They're staggering! Sterling flatware is a standard fixture at auctions. Usually it comes in a fine wooden chest, and almost without exception it sells for one-fifth to one-third of the retail price. We even saw one lovely sterling set in great condition go for less than the melt-down price for silver!

Look every piece over for scratches. The more ornate the design, the less the wear will show, and a little wear actually adds a mellow appearance to sterling. If a set is monogrammed, it will diminish the interest in it by a good deal. Since we find many of the monograms hard to read anyway, we can't fathom what difference it makes, but it does make a difference. You may find that several pieces are missing from a set. For instance, a service for twelve may have only eleven dinner forks, and nine soup spoons. This will deter many people—don't be one of them. If the pattern is still

Compatible, but different, spoon racks add interest to this dining room wall. The spoons are collector spoons but any attractive spoons will do. Both racks and spoons are frequent auction finds.

being made, you can fill in the gaps with new pieces. And if the pattern has been retired, there are entire businesses (usually advertised in antiques periodicals and decorating magazines) that stock out-of-production silver and dinnerware patterns. You may pay a bit more for this service than if you were able to buy your missing pieces new, but look what you're saving on the rest of the set.

American sterling is either marked "Sterling," "925," "925/1000," or "Sterling weighted." "Sterling" is the most common mark.

SPOONS. Between 1890 and sometime in the 1920s, traveling salesmen brought souvenir spoons home for their wives. People on vacations or just passing through an area found spoons inviting mementos of their trips. Some of these spoons were very ornate. Others were cheaply made and emblazoned with advertising pictures and slogans. These were given away by businesses. Other spoons depicted a town, state, or particular spot—such as a waterfall. Some spoons commemorated events. Perhaps the most common spoons are the presidential spoons—one for each president.

Limited edition spoons are more valuable than spoons that were widely produced if the quality is equal. A handle in the shape of a figure or design makes a spoon more desirable than it would be if the handle were plain or engraved. An intricately designed spoon bowl is a feature for which collectors look as is enamel. A spoon rack complete with a spoon collection, either of one specific type or a mixture, is a delightful touch to a kitchen or dining room wall.

SUMMING IT UP

The secondhand markets will yield everything you need for your kitchen and dining room. You can get beautiful plates and other useful items that have lost their mates. Using them together makes an interesting table setting, either in your kitchen or dining room. However, make this (what we call "a mix-match") serendipitous. It works best if plates and glasses are the same size and if the designs harmonize.

The suggestions in this chapter give just a smattering of the recycled articles you can use to add interest and elegance to the areas in which you dine and prepare food.

CHAPTER FIVE

Accessories: Little Things Mean a Lot

HAVE YOU EVER gone into a home where the furniture was well placed and the colors harmonized beautifully, but the whole package didn't seem to work? It was boring? Something was missing? Chances are the home lacked interest because it wasn't well accessorized or wasn't accessorized at all. It's those little or large, unusual or ordinary, useful or just ornamental pieces that make a place distinctive and charming. Virtually any surface is a possible site for accessorizing. The walls, the tables, a mantel piece, bookcases, and the floor all can be dressed up to add warmth and personality to a room.

MAKING IT INTERESTING

There are two main types of accessories: those that are attractive and also functional and those that are simply pleasing to look at. Books, candlesticks, and lamps are in the first category. Figurines, pictures, and commemorative plates fall into the second group. If a

Any dining room or kitchen table can be dressed up with the addition of a soup tureen.

"Terrific" is the only word to describe this Fritz and Floyd planter found in a one dollor box lot.

piece was once functional but you're using it only as a decoration, we would put it under the second category. Friends of ours have a splendid example of this—a horn from an Italian gondola. The horn hangs beside their fireplace and always brings comments from first-time guests. An old coffee grinder placed on a mantle or end table is a decorative use for an object that once had to earn its keep.

Whether you're accessorizing with a theme or in an eclectic manner, select each piece with an eye to the total look of the room. There should be a sense of continuity among the items that you're going to display together, either in a grouping or on the same piece of furniture. For instance, a piece of modern art glass will look incongruous on the same end table as a pair of oriental figurines done in 1950s style and an old majolica (tin glazed) plate. Any one of these things is desirable and would be interesting with more compatible pieces.

Perhaps no other area of decorating lends itself to the second-hand markets as much as accessorizing. Yard sales, garage sales, auctions, secondhand stores, you name it—are full of decorative items and articles that can be used as accessories. But before you embark on a search for objects to spruce up your environs, assess the space you have to accommodate them. And make a list of those articles that are needed for their function as well as eye appeal.

You may have a sofa that really needs the addition of a couple of pillows to be comfortable or a lamp at either end. The pillows and lamps go on your "Need" list. If there's smoking in your home, you need ash trays. You need a set of coasters to protect your table tops. You need things like wastebaskets. Then there are the artifacts which may or may not be utilitarian, but which are the glue that holds a decorating theme together. Among these might be vases, planters, wall pockets, candles and candleholders, statues, and so forth.

Except for the essentials, it's a mistake to form a hard-and-fast plan for accessorizing. You never know what wonderful things will materialize at the various sales, and you want to approach them with an open mind. While well-known name items such as a Roseville vase, a Limoges plate, or a Northwood carnival bowl may bring big bucks, most of the smaller, unknown articles, especially if they're newer, will sell for next to nothing when they're recycled.

On the other hand, you may want to set a definitive theme in a room. For instance, you may be drawn to anything that's Victorian, or your preference may run toward Art Deco, or the 1950s may fascinate you. While it will  take you a bit more time to furnish your castle in any one style or period, it certainly can be done with a little time and a lot of patience. And every time you find just the right item, the satisfaction is enormous.

The old and the new marry well if you observe a few basic rules. First, combining formal and informal accessories rarely works. Second, a clash of colors, whether it's in furniture or accessories, creates a discordant note in any decorating scheme. Purchase only articles that fit in with the hues you're using. Third, don't buy accessories that are so large they'll overpower other items in the room. A five-foot statue just doesn't go in a ten-foot by ten-foot room with diminutive furniture no matter how fine the statue may be and regardless of how good a buy it is.

As we've said earlier, most auction houses sell box lots—a number of items put together and sold as one lot. You get the whole thing—the good, the bad, and the indifferent. Almost always there's something that's good, and almost always it's accompanied by a lot of junk. If you root around in these lots before the auction begins, you may uncover items with great potential for use as accessories.

We've unearthed many a bargain this way. One lot held a 1939 World's Fair ashtray in mint condition; salt and pepper shakers in the form of cats; and a badly tarnished, sterling silver snuff box that was so tangled into a dirty, old Christmas garland that we didn't find it until we got home. The box also held two broken figurines, a soiled pot holder, and a small seascape that was too water stained to be salvaged. We paid $6 for the box. The ashtray is on the coffee table in our family room. The salt and pepper shakers are in our kitchen. (We're animal fanciers). We polished the snuff box and placed it on top of a Windsor desk, where it looks right at home with a vase and a slightly larger decorative box. We threw out the rest of the lot.

Be alert when you bid on box lots. There are auction goers who switch merchandise from one box to another. So you may look at box A, find just the right vase for your end table in it, get the box when it comes up for bid, and discover that the vase isn't there. It's wise to check the contents of any box lot in which your

This lovely Oriental silk was unframed when it was purchased in a box lot. The items on the mantel were acquired over time to complete the Oriental ambiance.

interested just before the auctioneer brings it up for sale. We've been stung this way more than once, and now we're super careful.

BUYING AND USING ACCESSORIES

The following is a list of the types of items you might find on the secondary markets and suggestions on how to buy and use them:

ADVERTISING MEMORABILIA. If a certain product is dear to your heart, advertising pieces from that company would be a good theme for a display in your home. For instance, there are many Coca Cola and Pepsi Cola items from trays to old bottles and bottle carriers, thermometers, bottle openers calendars, clocks, signs, toys, and myriad other things all sought by the collector. Some are quite common and widely reproduced. If you're a purist, you'll want originals and will have to pay a lot for them. But if a reproduction will satisfy you, you can assemble a collection for only a few dollars. Other beverage collectibles bear the emblems of Dr. Pepper, Moxie, and Anheuser-Busch.

Old tins which once held products are also very collectible. Gathered together, a few of these tins add a note of nostalgia to a family room or kitchen. Baking powder containers, tins that once held sewing machine oil, tobacco tins, etc. usually have great old graphics. Planters Peanuts had many forms of advertising gimmicks including salt and pepper shakers, peanut butter makers, ashtrays, and cracker jars. Some of these have been reproduced, others haven't.

If you're old enough to remember Nipper the RCA dog, you might want to include replicas of this famous pooch when you accessorize. Nipper can either be part of a dog collection or you can have an entire display of items that feature him. These include salt and peppers, statues (which are rare), signs, and pictures in which he was portrayed with his head cocked and his ear to the horn of a gramophone.

ART GLASS. Some wonderful examples of art glass turn up on the markets that feature recycled goods. (Most art glass is one-of-a-kind.) Old pieces, especially signed and dated examples, go through the roof. But simply lovely glass, from a more contemporary era, that is unsigned gets passed over by dealers and collectors. Even signed pieces that are newer often are shunned. There is a certain snobbery among collectors, and it works to the advantage of those of us whose goal is to furnish a home with attractive furniture and artifacts. When you purchase glass, in addition to looking for the signature and date, examine the piece to see if the glass is cloudy (or "tired" as it's commonly referred to). Signed or unsigned, dated or undated, a foggy piece of glass is unattractive.

You can show your art glass to advantage in several ways. A large art glass vase looks important on a desk, a table, on top of a television cabinet, etc. Or you may want to make an arrangement of vases in different sizes—perhaps in the same colors or maybe in a variety of complementary hues. A glass bowl is a fine choice for the centerpiece of a dining table where, depending on the shape of the bowl, you might want to fill it with fruit. If the bowl has matching candlesticks, so much the better. Epergnes (tiered glass bowls with several small vases or candleholders) are usually made of glass; and empty or filled with fresh flowers, an epergne makes a dramatic statement on a dining table. Glass bowls or epergnes also work well as the focal point of a coffee table.

BANKS. If you like money, and who doesn't, banks are fascinating collectibles. There are mechanical examples where you place a coin in a certain place, push or pull something, and the coin disappears into the bank. For instance, you might put a quarter on an elephants trunk, pull his tail, and the coin will go into his mouth. There are still banks, that (as the name implies) perform no action but often depict a place or thing. And then there are cash register banks that look and operate like a cash register. Many companies have used banks for advertising give aways. Of all the types of banks, we like the mechanicals the best. But, if you find one that looks shiny and new, that's probably because it is shiny and new—Don't pay a lot for it. These banks have been reproduced in great numbers.

BATH ACCESSORIES. A cluttered bathroom or vanity counter top will ruin the best decorating efforts. But there are several ways to organize this room. A hat box appropriately decorated can be used to hold items that tend to get scattered, or a lazy Susan or other type of turntable can be put to use keeping articles in one place. Items like this are often found in box lots. You can paint or paper them, using wallpaper or an adhesive backed covering. We know one man, a radio and phonograph collector, who has an old phonograph turntable in his bathroom on which he keeps his shaving stuff and other toiletries.

If your bathroom is small and has little storage space, you might want to suspend a wire basket from the ceiling. You can store soaps, aerosol cans, towels, and so forth in these baskets, freeing up counter space and making your bathroom look neat.

The supply of used curtain rods far exceeds the demand. This is because most people don't carry with them a list of measurements necessary for a purchase of this type. (A mistake we hope you won't make.) And curtain rods have uses other than for hanging curtains. Cafe rods, especially nice brass ones, can stand in for towel racks. They work well for guest towels which are smaller and weigh less than bath towels. If you have a large family and a large bathroom, try a drapery rod . There are some beautiful ones that you can buy very inexpensively.

Storing toothbrushes so they're at the ready can be a problem if you have company, if your family is a particularly large one, or if your bathroom doesn't have one of those built-in ceramic toothbrush holders. When we had more brushes than we had slots to keep them in, we bought an old pipe rack at a garage sale, scrubbed and painted it, and it held up to twelve toothbrushes. A smaller pipe rack would work well in a man's bathroom.

BOOKCASES. You may want bookcases that hold nothing but books, or you might want to display other accessories interspersed with your favorite volumes. We used to have a bookcase with a fish tank, flanked by books, on one of the middle shelves. The brilliantly colored tropical fish gave us (and our cats) many hours of pleasure. We probably would never have had fish if we hadn't come upon a 10-gallon tank with all the trimmings at a garage sale for only one dollar. Some bargains are just irresistible.

You might want to display a small print or oil painting on a shelf with a few books on one side of it. Whether you want one small bookcase or an entire wall of books, when you're planning your library, put large books on the lower shelves; books you use

Walls of books add a colorful note to any room. They can be purchased very inexpensively, often by the box, at auction.

frequently, such as reference books, on the shelf that's easiest to reach; and smaller books on upper shelves. You may prefer to group your books according to subject, but if your library is strictly for show, placing them according to size or color will work better for you.

BOOKENDS. Unusual bookends are frequent auction finds. We've been lucky enough to get some uncommon single examples in box lots. We put one end of a row of books against the side of the bookcase and hold up the other end with a single book end. Old bottles, vases, or other hollow articles make wonderful bookends if you fill them with sand; or you can also use almost any object, of the right size, that's heavy enough to support the weight of a few books. If your bookends are too light to do the job and get pushed aside by the weight of the books, put a piece of double-sided tape on the bottoms of the bookends to keep them in place.

BOOKS. Do you like to read? Have you ever dreamed of owning your own library? Are you in for a treat! Recycled books, unless they're first editions (and even a few of these slip through on occasion) can be yours for a fraction of the original price. Garage sales and flea markets sport an array of volumes from the latest in fiction to old, outdated encyclopedias. But at tag sales and auctions you'll find books by the carton going for as little as one dollar a box. We once sent eleven boxes of books to an auction, and the entire eleven boxes brought us only one dollar. Another mistake we'll never make again!

Although most modern books are sold individually when they're new, there was a time when books were bought in sets. These volumes were bound in fine leather and often had gilt pages and handsome end papers. Most were highly prized and kept in glass-fronted bookcases which protected the books. Because of this care, there are some fine old books in almost mint condition on the secondary markets.

You may want to have one wall of your living room or family room floor-to-ceiling books, you may want bookcases on either side of a fireplace or entertainment center. Or you may want just a small, freestanding bookcase or two strategically placed. A few books flanked by unusual bookends add a note of interest to a table or desk top. We prefer older books. They have so much more character than newer books, and they're still good reading. Although we confess that we haven't read all of the more than 1,500 volumes that grace our home.

BOXES. Available in a large variety of sizes and materials, boxes were made for almost endless purposes. Many of these containers have become decorative items. Crates displaying advertising for vegetables, fruits, ointments, medicines, cleaners, etc., are hot items with some people. They are used as decorative pieces or often as end or coffee tables. There are fine old knife boxes, tea boxes, handkerchief boxes, and glove boxes all of which can be used in decorative groupings. And, of course, cigarette and cigar boxes are a reminder of that not-so-distant time when smoking not only was politically correct, it was fashionable.

BUTTONS AND BOWS. Some accessories are real conversation pieces. For instance, you might chose to fill a frame with unusual, old buttons. These come up at auction on a regular basis. Often they're sold by the box and, unless there's a button collector in the audience, go for next to nothing. All lots of buttons aren't fascinating; but look closely, and you're apt to find beautiful enamel buttons, old military buttons, cameo buttons, and so forth mixed in with the mundane.

We've often found clip-on bows, the type ladies used to use to dress up their shoes, mixed in with buttons. One or several of these bows looks pretty clipped onto the edge of a dressing table mirror, especially in a teenage girl's room.

CANDLEHOLDERS. Few homes are without at least one pair of candleholders. Complete with candles, they're still almost obligatory to set the mood for a romantic dinner, but they also can add decorative touches throughout a home. And candle sticks are one of the most readily available items on the second-hand market. In pairs, depending on what they're made of, they often command high prices. But we think individual candle holders are more interesting, and they certainly are much cheaper. You might have just the spot for a collection of all brass candle holders of varying sizes. Fill them with candles of one color that matches something in the room or assign a different color candle to each candle holder. This is really eye-catching. Perhaps you don't care for brass but like the candle stick idea. How about a number of porcelain or glass examples? Why not mix the two? Or aim for all depression glass—maybe all pink or all blue. There are Carnival glass holders available, too. The variety in candle sticks is almost endless. You only need a good eye and a little imagination to get an impressive display.

CLOCKS. A standard item at almost all of the secondhand markets, clocks make a fun grouping. You can collect either small or large, standing or hanging examples. Although you want a display that's in balance, the sizes aren't as critical as they are if you're assembling a display of figurines. You could even make a variety of sizes an important feature of your collection. Used for this purpose, the clocks don't even have to work, which makes your job of finding them for a good price much easier. Or, if you find that your clocks are in working order and that they're from several different countries, how about setting each one at the time of its country of origin?

Some clocks chime, some have alarms, some tick loudly. Some are key wound, some electric, some battery operated. Specialize or generalize, and enjoy your collection.

COVERED DISHES. We were guests in a home where our hosts had a display of covered dishes on the sideboard in the dining room. These dishes each had a cover in the shape of an animal. Our friends said they'd been collecting covered dishes in animal shapes for several years. Some of the designs are quite common—others rare. The prices they bring reflects their availability. Westmoreland, McKee, and Indiana Tumbler and Goblet were the companies that manufactured most of the older examples. Kampl Glass Company began reproducing a cat, a fox, a rabbit, and a few others in the 1960s.

While chickens, hens, and cats appear on the market more frequently than other animal covered dishes, dogs, ducks, eagles, elephants, fish, fox, horses, lambs, lions, rabbits, and swans surface from time to time. Their scarcity makes them more desirable. Many of these dishes are white milk glass, but other colors in both milk glass and clear glass have been produced. New Westmoreland covered animal dishes (and other glass with the Westmoreland trade mark) glut the market. Although the company is no longer in business, other manufacturers have purchased their molds.

DECOUPAGE. If you like decoupage, the secondary markets should be heaven for you. They're full of inexpensive items that lend themselves to this form of decorating. Boxes, placemats, tables with damaged tops, trays, clocks, hurt lamp bases, lamp shades, and numerous other items can be refurbished in this manner. All you need is a paint brush, glue, varnish, a few old magazines, and an artistic flair. Simply cut out the designs that strike your fancy, glue them on the object to be decorated, allow the glue to dry well, and then apply several coats of lacquer, letting it dry thoroughly between applications.

FIGURINES. Groupings of figurines that fall into one category can make for a eye-pleasing display. There are many people who collect Hummel, Lladro, Staffordshire, or other well-known figurines and invest literally thousands of dollars in the small statues. These replicas command astronomical prices at auctions unless they're damaged. When this is the case, and it is usually the case with some pieces at an auction that features any popular collectible, the hurt figurines go for pennies on the dollar. While pricey figurines are fine, there are many other types and makes of figurines that are just as nice and much, much less expensive.

Figurines dubbed "Hummel-look-a-likes" glut the recycled markets, for instance. And there are other, inexpensive figurines depicting almost anything you might want to display. Lefton China Company has been in business since 1940 and makes ceramics in many forms. They're quite inexpensive, although Lefton is beginning to have a following among collectors.

Beswick, an English firm that was founded in the 1890s, has been producing mid-priced animal (and other) figurines since 1936. These replicas are finely detailed, are fairly easy to find, and are fun to collect if you're an animal lover. Dogs and cats are frequent and popular subjects. Some pieces are fairly expensive, but the quality is high and you may get a real buy because Beswick isn't as well-known as some other manufacturers. These figurines should appreciate in value, making your decorating dollar an investment. The company, which has been owned by Doulton since 1973, also makes a line of toby mugs. (Cups made in the shapes of heads and sometimes entire figures of people.)

If you decide you want a display of figurines, remember that size is important. Your arrangement of dogs will look pretty silly if you have a four-inch high poodle, a one-inch high German shepherd, and a five-inch high cocker spaniel sitting together on a table. Very small or miniature examples usually are most effective when they're kept either in a shadow box with shelves, a knick-knack shelf, or a small, glass front cabinet. They look lost on a table top or mantle.

HATBOXES. Time was when there were few households that didn't have an array of hatboxes. Now that few people wear hats, the boxes have been discarded, but they're being picked up at auctions and flea markets by people with an eye for decorating. Most of these boxes are made of stiff cardboard. Round examples seem to be more desirable than the square boxes, and a hatbox with the name of a favorite department or specialty store will command a high price from those with fond memories of that particular establishment. However, the preponderance of hat boxes sell cheap. Wallpapered or painted, they make a good showing in a bedroom or bathroom.

A few years ago we did an arrangement we particularly liked in a room with multicolored, floral wallpaper. We'd purchased a roll of rose-and-white striped wallpaper at an auction and papered three hatboxes, in graduated sizes (also an auction find) with it. The boxes were displayed piled up in the corner of the room. The rose on the boxes matched the rose in the floral wallpaper almost perfectly. Because there was only one double roll of wallpaper, the hammer price was a mere fifty cents.

We've seen hatboxes covered with plain paper and stenciled or handpainted. In our section of the country, Pennsylvania Dutch designs are favorites for this type of decorating.

INKWELLS. Some inkwells that are being recycled come from as far back as the era when quill pens were in use. They are fascinating additions for anyone who's enthusiastic about history or literature. You might want to have one on your desk, if you have an office at home. A display of several inkwells on an end table or library table in your living room will make a statement about your interests. There is a wide range of ink wells—from those with humble origins that were mass produced for members of the working class, all the way to hand wrought silver or gold examples crafted for monarchs. In between those two extremes, there are myriad ink wells fashioned from many materials, including glass, metal, porcelain, and wood in a variety of shapes. Inkwells are common on the secondhand markets. Their value varies wildly. But even a grouping of moderately priced examples makes a fine showing.

LIMITED EDITION COLLECTIBLES. Collector plates, statues, vases, figurines, and other limited edition items are found in great numbers at auctions, and unless there's a collector on hand, they sell for cents on the dollars they originally cost. For instance, collector plates rarely bring more than five dollars, and we've seen them sell for as little as two dollars. These are plates that originally cost upwards of thirty dollars! If you like this sort of thing, you can either display them in a china cabinet or hang them on a wall. Other limited edition collectibles can spark up a room either displayed in groups or individually.

LINENS. You can refinish a dresser or table with a less-than-perfect top or you can cover it attractively and no one but you need be aware of the flaw. Linens, including some lovely dresser scarves, are sold by the box at auctions. Many of these linens are hand embroidered, others are decorated with lace; some are crocheted, and some are plain. The handwork runs the gamut from expert to amateur. Few of these box lots sell for more than a pittance at an auction. We often feel sad thinking of the hours spent doing all that work which is now ranked so low on the scale of desirability. Most of the linens will look tired and dusty when you purchase them, but a good cleaning will spruce them up. Scarves that were fashioned to be worn either around the neck or on the head can be used on furniture tops as well. You'll find them in everything from cotton to silk, square to oblong, dressy to primitive. We used to have a lovely square, paisley silk scarf on one of our bedroom dressers. The length was just right, but it was too wide. After folding it in half and pressing it, we had a beautiful cover for the not-so-beautiful top we were trying to mask.

Antimacassars protected the arms and backs of chairs from dirt and the oily hair dressings that were common in the first half of the 20th century. These small pieces of crocheted, embroidered, or otherwise decorated material add a touch of authenticity to a room furnished in 1920s or 1930s fashion.

MAGAZINES. Like books, magazines add hominess to a room if they're situated neatly on a coffee table, in an attractive magazine rack, or other suitable place. Too often, however, magazines get strewn around on table tops, making the room look more cluttered than charming. Magazines from the early 1900s are frequent finds on the secondhand markets. As with all paper goods, smell them before you buy them. Most have been stored either in attics or basements and have that impossible-to-get-rid-of musty odor—not a plus for anyone's living room! But there are old magazines and periodicals out there that have been lovingly preserved.

In selecting magazines, look for those with graphics that appeal to you and, if possible, reflect your areas of interest.

MAGAZINE RACKS. Not so many years ago, every home boasted a magazine rack or two. People read more because there was little television. Most families subscribed to at least a few magazines which were eagerly awaited each month, especially by housewives. While most households still have magazines, they're considered throw-away items and so there are few new magazine racks. Those that are available from retail stores seem sadly lacking in character. If you're a magazine reader, especially one who can't bear to part with your magazines, interesting recycled racks await you.

Although there are some handsome examples of magazine racks, there are also other items that make excellent holders for magazines—a doll cradle is perfect for digest-size magazines, a baby cradle does the job for larger magazines and periodicals. Placed by a fireplace, a cradle will set the tone for the entire room. Stain it or paint it to match your color scheme. If you're fortunate enough to find an old wire egg basket, the type that held eggs in layers and had individual holes about the size of the eggs, you can store your magazines in it by rolling them up and inserting them where the eggs were held. Your magazine rack may not be one-of-a-kind, but it certainly won't be common either. A large wicker basket can hold many magazines, too.

MILITARY MEMORABILIA. Guns, swords, spent hand grenades, and replicas of cannons, while primarily "guy things," are hot collectibles. If you're a military or history buff, they may appeal to you, and they're certainly out there. In fact, entire auctions are dedicated to them. You may find a Civil War rifle and a sword from the Spanish American War being auctioned off along with more modern pieces. Some people dedicate an entire room to this type of memorabilia, while others simply have one piece, such as a sword, hanging on a wall or over a mantle. Auctions are certainly your best source for weapons, but you'll find that in some states you can't take possession of any type of gun until there's been a background check. The auctioneer will put the gun away for you if yours is the winning bid. Usually you can get it within a few days. We caution you that it's generally unsafe to fire an antique gun. They're just for display.

OIL LAMPS. If the surroundings of our early ancestors fascinate you, consider a collection of oil lamps. There are many types. Some, which have handles, are called "finger lamps." They're generally more expensive than those without handles, which are made to be kept in one spot. Oil lamps come in a variety of sizes, from miniature to quite large. Some of them are in wall brackets—a pair of these looks great over a mantle. Occasionally, you may see colored glass oil lamps. Cobalt blue examples bring big bucks.

In one home we visited, we were impressed with the owners' vast collection of oil lamps which were displayed on a shelf that ran all around the room, about two feet below the ceiling. There's no way a power outage is going to leave these people in the dark!

PILLOWS. We were at an auction with a friend one day, when he bid on a truly disreputable-looking sofa. The frame was beat up, one arm had stuffing coming out of it and the other was threadbare, and the cushions were stained. When he got the sofa for five dollars, we thought he was out of his mind. No one likes a good buy better than we do, but there are limits! Of course, we were too polite to comment. A few weeks later when we were guests in our friend's home, we noticed three floor pillows in a charming blue-and-gold pattern. He chuckled as he told us that these were from the sofa he'd purchased. He'd discarded everything but the cushions, which his wife had re-covered and which were a handsome and useful addition to their family room. If you could use extra seating, but don't have room for more chairs and sofas, you might want to consider floor pillows.

Throw pillows also perk up a room, adding a luxurious look to beds, chairs, and sofas. They're often available by the box at auctions or for a dollar or two at garage sales. Before you buy them, smell them to be sure they're not musty or mildewed. If the covers don't work for you, re-covering them is one of the easiest sewing jobs there is. If they have zippered covers, so much the better. You can remove and launder them.

PLANT STANDS. Plants, which do appear on the secondary market (although infrequently), have been a decorative standby for years. Displaying them innovatively is a talent, and plant stands of all descriptions glut the auction and garage sale markets. Some are standing, some hang on walls, some have several tiers and hold many plants, others will accommodate only one pot. Then there are items that were intended for other purposes that convert nicely into plant stands. A step ladder, painted to fit into your decorating theme, will hold many plants. Put a fairly large one on the bottom step and work down in size as you go up the ladder so that you have several small plants on the top. Or one large plant with long tendrils, such as a fuchsia or an ivy, looks dramatic when it's positioned on the top of the ladder and cascades down almost to the floor. A bookcase can be used to hold plants, too, but the plants should be turned regularly so that they get even light.

POTS. We dislike the plastic pots that frequently hold lovely plants. There are many attractive, inexpensive alternatives. Old water pitchers, the type that are part of a pitcher and basin set used for bathing in the days before indoor plumbing, make attractive planters. If you want one that's perfect, you're going to have to pay a premium, but like so many old items, these pitchers weren't gently used and many have chips and cracks. Others have lost their mates and along with them their desirability for antiques collectors. These hurt or lonely pitchers don't bring much money. Minor chips, or even some major ones, shouldn't detract from their usefulness as planters; but beware of cracks that water may leak through if a pitcher is converted to a planter.

Used canisters, especially those that aren't really old, can be picked up cheap, painted or wallpapered, or used as is for planters. Chipped cups or those without saucers provide attractive receptacles for small plants, such as African violets. There are some beautiful bone china tea cups to be had that fit nicely into formal rooms. A display of these cups, resplendent with small plants, is pleasing to plant lovers. If you have the saucers, so much the better. Less elegant cups make handy holders for plants on a kitchen window sill.

Wastebaskets come in many sizes and shapes and serve plants of corresponding sizes nicely. When converting anything to a planter, keep in mind that plants don't do well if their roots are sitting in water. We always put a layer of small or crushed stones, for drainage, in the bottom of containers we're using as planters.

Bird cages aren't just for the birds—they're great for housing potted plants, especially those with long, hanging tendrils. You'll find them in an array of materials including brass, gilt metal, wicker, and wood. Some are old, some new. Some are fine for use as a planter just as you find them, others need a coat of paint to spruce them up. We think this is a wonderful way for people with pets to also enjoy plants. Cats and dogs can't get by the caging to dig in the dirt and chew the leaves.

POTTERY. Weller, Red Wing, Roseville, and pottery from other well-known makers commands high prices (unless you stumble on a piece at a garage sale where the owner doesn't know what the

Many slightly damaged pieces can be had for a tiny percent of their worth if perfect. This hand-painted Limoges bowl, for example, has a small rim chip that's easily hidden by turning the chip tward the wall.

piece is), but fine pottery items from lesser-known or amateur potters draws very little interest from the buying public. At one auction, we picked up about twenty bowls and vases that were made by one such potter. They're delightful. Each one has the date it was made and the weather on that day incised in the bottom of the piece along, with the potter's name. We paid from one to three dollars for each one. What a buy!

QUILTS. Old quilts, hand sewn by ladies long ago, are prized for their designs and handwork. In the days of quilting bees, women took great pride in their ability to sew small, uniform stitches. Of course, there's a great deal of diversity in the quality of both the fabrics and the work in these quilts. There are many standard, recognizable designs—log cabin, daisy and oak leaf, and wedding ring are just a few of them.

If you're interested in a quilt, old or more recent, give it the smell test. Examine every inch of the quilt. The fabric may be rotting, especially where the quilt has been folded. If you're planning to use the quilt as a bedspread (and they are very attractive used in this manner with or without a bed skirt), measure it to be sure that the quilt in question is large enough to do the job.

The use of quilts isn't limited to bed covers. Quilt fanciers hang them on walls, use them as tablecloths, or throw them over the backs of sofas. Among the old, strongly desired quilts you find at auction, you'll probably encounter some that are machine sewn and obviously not as old. As a rule, quilt fanciers and dealers avoid these and you may be able to pick one up for just a few dollars. Although they don't bring with them the feeling of history you get with an older quilt, they're often in better condition and many of them are very attractive and mimic the patterns of older quilts.

SCREENS. Folding screens, both old and new, can be used to separate a room into two sections; to create a cozy corner for reading, a hobby or craft, or just a place to escape from the rigors of a busy household. Some screens are made entirely of wood. Others have wooden frames and fabric for the bodies of the screens. An old folding screen in good condition probably will bring a high price at auction. But many, if not most, of the screens on the secondary markets aren't in good condition. You may find that the fabric has rotted or, if the body of the screen is wood, that the main section is warped. Replacing fabric is easy. In fact, you'll probably be happier with the screen because it will reflect your taste in decorating and fit into your home better. Wallpaper will cover a multitude of problems on a wooden screen, and, again, you can select a pattern that suits your taste. If you have talent as an artist, use a wooden screen as your canvass. The results could be charming and personal, and you'll have a one-of-a-kind screen.

We've also seen folding screens used effectively as headboards. If you plan to do this, be sure that the screen is large enough for your mattress. A screen that's too large will work and provide a background for night stands or whatever you have beside your bed, but a screen that's skimpy, even if it's only an inch or two too narrow, will look makeshift. If you have a king-size bed, you may find two small screens with identical frames and finish them with the same wallpaper or fabric—perhaps matching your bedspread. You can fasten them together in the back, unobtrusively. Or you may prefer to tie them together with a ribbon, ties fashioned from the material you've used, or with tassels such as those that are sold to tie back drapes.

SPORTS COLLECTIBLES. If you're a sports enthusiast, why not make sports the theme for your family room? Old skis or snow shoes hung on a wall, wooden sleds or old ice skates beside a fireplace make a statement about a home's inhabitants. These items don't have to be antiques to bring a feeling of by-gone days to your decor. In one home we visited, the owners had a bicycle-built-for-two hanging over the sofa in their family room. It was the focal point and gave interest to what otherwise would have been a rather ordinary setting. Other friends of ours who are hockey buffs have two crossed hockey sticks adorning one wall. They bought them both at a garage sale for under a dollar.

TAPESTRIES. Old tapestries also make fantastic wall hangings or, if you find a particularly long one, you might want to use it as a dresser scarf or a runner on your dining room table. Look for bright colors. Many tapestries have faded over the years. Check the front coloring against the back. They should match in terms of hue. Some fading may be acceptable to you, but you don't want a tapestry that's lackluster and colorless.

Tapestries were made depicting everything from wars to romance. Since they're plentiful, you should be able to find examples that portray a subject that will fit into your home.

TRAYS. Large and small toleware trays (made of sheet metal and then painted) go high if they're old, original toleware dating from the early to mid 1800s. These handpainted treasures have a dull unvarnished finish. More modern toleware, the kind that can slip by for pennies, is usually stenciled and often has gold trim and a shiny finish. The loveliness of any toleware depends on the degree of talent the artist who executed the design possessed.

Other trays also make colorful and useful accessories. There are trays with glass tops that cover (often three dimensional) designs—fashioned from feathers, but-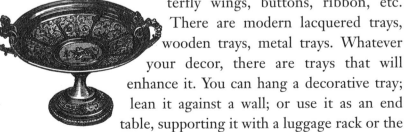terfly wings, buttons, ribbon, etc. There are modern lacquered trays, wooden trays, metal trays. Whatever your decor, there are trays that will enhance it. You can hang a decorative tray; lean it against a wall; or use it as an end table, supporting it with a luggage rack or the legs from an old television table. If you're clever with wood, you can fashion a stand for your tray.

VINTAGE CLOTHING. Do you love old Victorian dresses, top hats, and high button shoes? There's no reason you can't include vintage clothing in your decorating plan. Try draping an old piece of lingerie on a bedroom chair, or put hooks on your bedroom wall on which to display a vintage tux and a lovely old evening gown on hangers. An entry hall will be enlivened if you hang an old velvet cape and perhaps a muff where they'll be the first things seen when anyone enters the home. How about a pair of long white gloves with pearl buttons draped over a book on an end table in the living room?  Or an early 20th century bathing suit on a mannequin in your family room? A Victorian parasol, a child's dress and lacy bonnet, a silk waist coat, or a beaded evening bag can be used to accessorize your home.

BREAKING THE RULES

After having given you a few rules to follow in your accessorizing, we should now advise you that if you can get the results you want—fashion a room that pleases you—by breaking a few decorating rules, go right ahead. These rules are meant to be guidelines. They're what works most of the time. Only you know what works for you in your home. When you're viewing articles in the secondary markets, remember that an ugly duckling can turn into a beautiful swan with a touch of creativity.

CHAPTER SIX

Tips on Repairing and Cleaning

MERCHANDISE that is being sold for the second time, whether its described as recycled, second-hand used, gently used, formerly owned, pre-owned, or well loved, rarely comes flawless. Even brand-new articles are often damaged. In your sojourn through the used markets you may find an object that's just what you've been looking for, but it's damaged or covered with grime. Appraise it. Without a great deal of work you may be able to revive it.

We've learned a good deal about repairing and picked up many cleaning tips over the years. A rub here or dab there often will restore an item to (at least) acceptable and often like-new condition. We've tried to keep the procedures in this chapter simple, and the necessary tools and supplies limited. It's our belief that you don't have to be a professional to restore a piece to usefulness or enhance its appearance. If you can tighten a screw with a screwdriver, smooth a rough spot with sandpaper or steel wool, and apply paint with a brush or aerosol-spray can, you'll do just fine.

A little TLC turned this rocking chair from an eyesore into a conversation piece.

APPLIANCE REPAIRS

We'll assume that the large appliances you buy secondhand are mechanically sound, their motors, heating or cooling units work fine, and the only problem is that there are some scratches or other signs of wear on the exterior finish. To cover these blemishes, there are appliance touch-up enamels that come in small bottles with a brush in the cap (like the bottles of fingernail polish) available from hardware stores. The range of colors is good, but dabs of paint over a finish are usually obvious. A better choice is the enamel that comes in small aerosol cans, if you can find the color you want. If you can only find the color you need in the small bottles, consider using the spray unit described under *China and Pottery* repairs. You may want to repaint the whole surface. This will allow you to select a new color. The larger aerosol spray cans of paint recommended for appliances are the best choice. Remember to remove or cover with paper and masking tape any areas you do not want to paint.

If you're really bold, you can apply fabric panels to the appliance. The material should be soil resistant or easily cleaned. Better yet, washable wallpaper is easier to work with and apply. First cut out a paper pattern to insure a good fit. If you're using fabric, apply it with a spray-on glue that specifies on the label it will adhere to both fabric and metal. For wallpaper, use a contact glue spread on the underside of the paper with a brush. Before you buy spray-on glue, read the instructions for applying it. Some of these glues are not permanent, and others must be applied within a minute of spraying it in order to bond permanently.

MENDING HURT ACCESSORIES

BONE AND IVORY. For the most part, objects of bone and ivory should be left alone unless they are badly damaged. Old items of these materials may well show a few nicks or scratches, but the scars of time don't take from their value. If the piece is badly damaged, you can use paraffin to enhance its appearance and protect it from further deterioration. To fill cracks, pre-warm the piece with a hair dryer or leave it sitting in front of a heat outlet. The piece should be warm, not hot. Melt a chunk of a crayon that matches the piece in a double boiler or a small tin within a pot of water. Warning: Crayons are made of paraffin, and paraffin is highly flammable. Keep a box of baking soda (to extinguish an open flame) and the pot's lid (to contain the flame and prevent fresh oxygen from reaching it) by the stove before you heat the paraffin. Hot paraffin or wax will give a nasty burn if it splatters on your skin, so work carefully. When the crayon has melted, apply it to the cracks with an artist brush. To dispose of the leftover paraffin, pour it onto a thick layer of newspaper, let it harden, and throw it out.

If the bone or ivory piece is in danger of breaking apart, as a result of having dried out, and become brittle, it can be sheathed in a thin coat of paraffin. Heat the paraffin (sold in grocery stores for canning), following the instructions given in the previous paragraph. When the wax has liquefied, remove the double boiler from the stove and holding the pre-warmed piece with tongs dip half of it into the wax. Pull it out and let it cool, then dip the other half. Hold the piece over the pot for a few second after each dip to allow the excess paraffin to run off. The surplus wax that accumulates at each end of the piece can be easily trimmed off with a knife after the wax has completely cooled. The final step is to buff the piece. It is now better protected against the perils of handling.

CHINA AND POTTERY. You may buy a piece of china or pottery or an entire set at auction and learn after a closer examination that there are breaks, chips, cracks, or dings. This is discouraging. But take heart—there is a very good chance you can reclaim your purchase by repairing it.

Cups with handles broken off, plates that were dropped, and decapitated figurines, are only a few of the items that can be restored—if the pieces are there. Work with a glue that lists china and pottery among the materials it will bond. The pieces must be clean, and fit together snugly.

The main cause of sloppy glue jobs is misalignment. To avoid that error, before you start working, create a place and means to support the piece while it dries. This could be anything from a flat surface to a sculptured cradle. The former is easy, the latter requires some preparation. In most cases, a gluing box is the answer. It's not difficult to make one out of a cut-down cardboard box that is larger than the object you are going to repair. The depth should accommodate 5 or 6 inches of filler plus the object. The fill can be rice or clean, dry sand. (Beach and backyard sand isn't clean, it should be purchased at an aquarium supply store.) Mold a resting place in the fill by embedding a duplicate of the object, like a good one of a pair, or another plate of the same size, or lacking either of those, fashion the shape by hand. If there are more than two pieces to glue, do only two at a time. It'll be much easier to align the pieces and move the object into the cradle.

For items that are too small, or for some reason don't lend themselves to the gluing box, try floral clay. Its made of plastic, won't harden, and is reusable. Mold a cradle in the clay and line it with plastic wrap.

Yet another way to hold small objects together is to tape them to a support item with masking tape.

Handles, finials, pedestals, and other appendages that are being glued back in place must be held in there with as much pressure as possible. This can usually be done with masking tape. Run the tape over the object from top to bottom and side to side as an + or an x. It takes three hands, so you will need help.

Whatever means you use to support the object, be sure all excess glue is wiped from it before it's secured to the support and left to set.

Nicked edges and small chips can be filled with plaster of Paris mixed with white glue. The raw edges must be clean, which may require scraping or sanding. Your gluing box or other means of holding the object should be prepared. The glue and plaster of Paris mixture should be near to peanut butter consistency—it should cling to a knife blade. Begin patching as soon as it's mixed, because it sets up quickly. Plaster shrinks as it dries, therefore you must apply it generously. (In this case too much is a good thing.) After it dries, you can carefully sand the excess and shape it to the desired contours.

If you want to save the container in which you mixed the plaster, wash it out immediately after you have applied the plaster or it will set fast and hard and you'll have to soak, and then chisel or sand it out.

After the plaster has dried for a few hours, you can shape the patch. Carefully scrape off excess plaster that is on the surrounding area, or it will cause chunks of the patch to break off. Shape the patch with sandpaper—course for roughing out the contours, and fine for the finish. For a really smooth finish, follow up by rubbing the patch with your naked finger tips.

Epoxy putty—glue with filler—can be used for large repairs on China or any other material, except glass (unless it's painted). This terrific substance can be molded, sawed, filed, drilled, and painted. It comes in metal or wood tones. It dries in 1-1/2 hours and cures to a steel-like hardness in 12 hours. We've used it on damaged vases, bisque figurines, wood carvings, metal lamps, and furniture.

Like other epoxy products, it comes as two packages, the resin, and the hardener—each a different color. To mix, cut off or scoop out equal amounts from the two portions and roll and knead them together with a nail or stick to form a uniform-colored mass.

To shape, fill, or smooth it, work with your fingers dipped in soapy water. The putty doesn't shrink, so make the patch the finished size. As mentioned before, it can be filed or sanded, so rough spots can be refined after the epoxy cures. If it needs further smoothing, use an extra-fine grade of silicone carbide cloth.

As paint ages, its color alters, due to oxidation and exposure to light and pollutants. If the surface the patch is in has not been recently painted, we'd advise you to test the match by painting a piece of wood or paper first. After the test piece has dried, compare it with the paint surrounding the patch. If the color is off, blend in a few drops of white or black as needed. Choose the right finish—flat, semi-gloss, or high gloss. Apply the paint the consistency of nail polish—just thick enough not to run. Feather the edges so the two paints blend without a noticeable ridge. To do this, lightly brush from the center of the patch to the edge, then without pausing, sweep the brush up and off the surface. If a second coat is needed, slightly overlap the first coat with the same procedure to avoid a ridge.

Artist brushes work well for touch ups and small paint jobs. For larger jobs, we prefer a sprayer. We're not suggesting a sophisticated unit that costs mega-bucks. What we use is a simple, small paint spraying unit similar in application to the elements used by professional graphic artists. Professional units require an air compressor and come with a variety of nozzles that are not needed for touch ups, and they begin at around 50 dollars. Our small inexpensive unit was picked up at a craft supply store for under 15 dollars. Instead of a compressor, our sprayer uses an aerosol can of compressed air. The aerosol can with nozzle has a siphon tube at the bottom which lowers into a 16-ounce jar. When the air supply is used up, only the aerosol portion needs replacing. Sans the jar, it costs a little less than the complete unit. Paint used in a sprayer requires thinning with water or paint thinner—the paint label will tell you which to use. If you do a lot of spraying, this unit is clearly not the best choice. And standard aerosol cans of spray, if you can find the right color, are cheaper. But for an occasional touch up job, we think it's a good investment.

To date, all of our touch ups have required only a few ounces of paint, so we have inserted a smaller jar within the 16-ounce jar. If there is paint left over, we screw on a lid and keep it for another time. This eliminates having to clean the larger jar. (We trimmed off about a quarter-inch of the siphon tube to accommodate the smaller jar.)

CLOCK REPAIRS. Our clock-works repairs are confined to replacing damaged hands and missing pendulums (when there was one). If it's overwound or otherwise damaged, we advise you to consult a professional clock repair person. However, repairing and replacing parts to the case, where possible, is certainly within the ability of the amateur. Broken glass and other parts of the case may be mended or replaced. If the case is of wood, such as a mantle or grandfather clock, it can be repaired and refinished following the instructions given under the section on wood finishing later in this chapter.

Professional clock repairs and the replacement of original-type works can be expensive. However, there is a less costly approach to replace a damaged works, that is to use the working mechanism from a clock with a severely damaged case.

CRYSTAL AND OTHER GLASS

As dealers, we have seen a lot of mended glassware, most of it so sloppily repaired that it stood out like a bandaged thumb. With a little care, many of these pieces could have been fixed so that the mend would be unnoticeable without a close inspection. We define sloppy repairs as those that are out of alignment and/or show excess glue around the mend. Avoid these two mistakes and your chances of a good repair will rise from impossible to probable.

Most glass is transparent and will show cracks or mended joints, with the exception of applied handles and other appendages. In the case of good crystal, even a piece with a crack or other imperfection will retain a good percentage of its perfect-condition value. If you have a glass piece that you admire—regardless of its monetary value—it's worth repairing if possible, so you can continue to enjoy its beauty.

To glue broken glass follow the directions for gluing *China and Pottery* given earlier in this chapter.

Glass is a unique material and under certain conditions will flow—that is, heat can soften glass and cause it to expand into a crack or chip in its surface. Shallow cracks and pits in auto windshields are repaired by chemical treatments that utilize this unusual characteristic. We've not been able to locate one of these chemical kits—apparently they are not available to the general public. However, light scratches in glass can be flowed out with "jeweler's rouge." This is a reddish-colored, low-abrasive paste used to polish brass and other metals. It's available in hardware and hobby supply stores. Apply the rouge on a rag with a fingertip and rub the scratch. Your rubbing should be energetic enough to warm the glass.

Small nicks on the edges of goblets and other vessels can be sanded out. Starting with medium-course emery cloth, sand across the nick—following the curvature of the rim. The goal is to wear down a small area on each side of the nick and form a slight dip that eliminates the nick. The deeper the nick, the longer the length of surface you should grind down. When the nick is no longer noticeable, switch to a fine-grain emery cloth and sand the rim as smooth as the emery will allow. Move on to garnet paper and polish until the rim's surface shows no lines. Finish off with a powdered abrasive—such as pumice or rottenstone. The powder must be made into a paste. To do this, wrap a soft cloth around your finger tip and dampen it with baby oil or a cooking oil, and pat on some of the abrasive. Rub the rim in one direction (non circular) and apply more abrasive or oil as needed. Keep polishing until the area looks and feels as smooth as the rest of the rim. Under close examination, the altered section will look slightly

cloudy compared to the rest of the rim. This dullness can be eliminated, or nearly so, by rubbing the rim with jewelers rouge. If you
have a small rotary tool (electric drill), the work of grinding and
polishing will go considerably faster. All the abrasive products
mentioned above are available at your local hardware store.

Nicks in figurines, bowls, and other ornate glass pieces can be
made to disappear, or be less obtrusive, by the same grinding and
buffing technique as above. We purchased a signed R. Lalique
(expensive and highly sought) crystal bird at a house auction a few
years ago. The bird's wings were extended as in flight, and the tip
of one of the wings was chipped. We sanded and polished the nick
into oblivion and sold it to a collector who, aware of the repair,
was happy with his purchase. The selling price was less than ten
percent below what it would have gone for perfect .

We've seen a hundred, maybe more, cut or pressed glass bowls
and sugar and creamers with scalloped or serrated rims. Perhaps
ninety percent of them had one or more broken off "teeth." We've
not bothered repairing the pressed bowls, but we have worked on
several cut-glass bowls. The glass is thick, which requires more
sanding and polishing, but the modified teeth blend into the *busy*
rim so well they are difficult to spot.

LAMPS

There are some interesting, even exotic, lamps on the used market, lamps you will never see in a new furniture store. However
fancy or plain, the lamp you bought, or are contemplating buying,
may require mending or upgrading for safety—which usually can
be done easily. To replace worn or damaged electric parts, first
consider the structure of a typical single-bulb table lamp.

From the bottom up, in order: Base, center pipe, harp retain-
er, socket cap, socket, insulating sleeve, socket's outer shell, harp
with threaded bracket, shade, finial. The electric cord enters at the
lower end of the base, rises through the center pipe, and attaches

Here's a Martha Washington sewing stand bought at auction. It's topped with one of a pair of signed, French, turn-of-the-century cherub lamps found in disrepair at a flea market. A good cleaning, a little artists' wax, and a pair of shades and the lamps were perfect for our bedroom.

to the socket. In some lamps there is no center pipe, in others there is no harp—the shade has wire loops that squeeze over the light bulb. In lamps that have two light bulbs, a bracket screws on to the top of the center pipe in place of a harp.

Worn cords and sockets are the most common problems with older lamps. If the lamp has a fabric-covered cord (that is not obviously new—they're still available), replace it.

To replace a lamp cord (which is unplugged): 1—Unscrew the finial and lift off the shade. 2—Remove the harp by squeezing its lower prongs, if there are retaining sleeves over the prongs, you must first slide them up. 3—If the lamp has a felt pad at the bottom of the base, pry it off. 4—If the cord has a loop in it, work the loop several inches toward the plug end. 5—If there is a set screw at the bottom of the socket, remove it. 6—Unscrew the socket from the center pipe. This will twist the cord inside the pipe, but it should freely pivot at the bottom end. 7—Pull the socket and cord up three or four inches from the center pipe. 8— Remove the outer shell of the socket by squeezing it where it is marked to do so and slipping off the shell. 9—A paper insulating tube covering the socket should be visible; remove it. 10—The socket has two terminals (screws), a silver one and a brass one. The stripped ends of the cord are wrapped around these posts. Untwist them and the socket is free. (If the socket needs replacing, this is the time to do it.)

The new cord you are installing must have the ends stripped of its rubber insulation—just as the old wire protruding from the center pipe has. With the old cord as your guide, part and strip an end of the new cord. There are special pliers-type tools, available at hardware stores, to strip off the ends, but you can do it with a pocketknife. First, separate the end of the cord, as the original one is. Cut the tip and pull the two strands apart. Then place one of the strands between a knife blade and your thumb and roll it. Use only enough pressure to cut through the rubber insulation, and not the wire. The cut should be the same distance from the end as the original wire. Repeat the procedure with the second strand. The section of the cord's insulation you have just cut should slide off easily. If not, carefully slice it lengthwise and pull it off.

There are two ways to insert the new cord into the center pipe: Pull the old cord out and feed the new one in or attach the new cord onto the old one and pull the new one in as you pull the old one out. The problem with the former way is that the longer the center pipe, the more difficult it is to feed the wire all the way through it—it snags on the inner wall of the pipe. When we've had this problem, we have lowered string with a weight at the end through the pipe, and then pulled the attached cord on through.

It's best to attach either the new cord or string to the old cord before pulling it out. With some lamps, the center pipe is so narrow that it can't accommodate the additional bulk of string. We've found that you can puncture a hole near the end of each wire and secure them butted together with a small piece of wire and pull them through.

With the new wire in place, make an underwriters knot (form a loop in each of the two strands were they divide. Pass the remaining wire from each loop through the other loop and tighten it) which will prevent the cord from being pulled loose from the socket at the plug end. Attach the two wires, silver on silver and brass on brass, and assemble the lamp in the reverse order that you used to take it apart.

Attaching a plug to the cord is easy. There are four types of plugs: 1—The manufacturer's plug molded to the cord. 2—The old fashioned, round ones, where the cord passes through the center of the plug and its ends wrap around terminals. 3—The clamp-style plug that has a shell with prongs you pinch open and pull free to insert the tip of the blunt-cut cord, then squeeze the prongs back together and back into the shell. 4—The snap-on plug, which has a lever on the top or side. Lift the lever and insert the cord about 1/4 inch and close the lever. With both the clamp-style and the snap-on plugs, closing them pushes teeth (small spikes) into the wire for the needed contact.

All the parts that are needed to rewire lamps are available at hardware stores. However, although we frequently repair or replace lamp parts, we find everything we need in the secondhand markets. Here's our secret:

Ugly lamps, regardless of age or condition, are difficult, if not impossible, to sell at auctions. We buy them when our parts supply is running low. Twenty-five cents to a dollar is the range we pay. These horrid lamps contain five to ten dollars, sometimes more, worth of good usable parts. Why? Some of these lamps have finials that are unattainable any other way. Some lamps are damaged but have lovely shades of silk or other quality materials.

If you have a lamp with a shade that fits too high or too low, you can buy a new shade, replace the harp with one taller or shorter, or, if it's too low, add an extender/riser—an attachment similar in appearance to a small brass finial. It screws on to the top of the harp where the finial goes, the shade's ring fits on it, and the finial screws through the ring into the riser.

FURNITURE AND OTHER WOOD OBJECTS

For the most part, furniture is made of wood, and wood is usually easier to repair than metal, glass, or plastic. Of course, other things are made of wood too, such as boxes, figures, dishes, bowls, canes, trays, gun stocks, and lamp bases. The list could go on, but the basic approach to repairing or cleaning almost any piece of wood is the same, repair the damage and restore the site to normal. The biggest difference between items made of wood isn't size or use but the finish. Surfaces covered with gold leaf, paint, or varnish must be finished off differently, but the repair of the underlying wood, whether it is a wood table or a box in which to store a chess set, is basically the same.

Different Woods

There are two types of wood, softwood and hardwood. Softwood comes from coniferous trees such as, cedar, Douglas fir, hemlock, pine, redwood, and spruce. These trees grow faster and are more plentiful than hardwoods, and their wood is cheaper.

SOFTWOOD. Less durable than most hardwood, softwood is easier to cut and shape and not likely to split when a nail or screw is driven into it. Lumber yards and home repair centers carry a wide assortment of softwood boards in different grades. The grades are based on appearance; that is, the number of flaws that are in the board, such as knots and gashes.

HARDWOOD. Comes from deciduous trees that include ash, birch, cherry, mahogany, maple, oak, teak, and walnut. These trees take longer to mature than conifers and therefore are more costly. Their wood is also stronger and longer lasting than the softwoods, and their grains and hardness provide more desirable surfaces. Because hardwoods are prone to split along their grains, it's best to pre-drill before inserting screws or large nails. Saw blades and drill bits must be sharp to cleanly penetrate these woods. Lumber sup-

pliers carry a limited variety and supply of hardwood. However, they will usually special order specific boards for you.

Damages and Remedies

Most furniture and other household items made of wood are enhanced and preserved with a multi-coat finish. After the final sanding, apply single coats (listed in the order of application) of sealer, stain, sealer, topped with varnish, or lacquer, or shellac, or more recently, polyurethane. In some cases, a light sanding is required between coats. A one-step finish is an alternative to the traditional one just given. Apply oil mixed with varnish or polyurethane directly to the sanded, bare stained surface. This finish is simple and quick, but doesn't penetrate the wood as deeply nor look as rich as the multi-coat finish. A third finish can be achieved by applying paste wax directly over the stained surface. Wax buffed into the wood's pores provides a hard, durable finish. You'll need to reapply it periodically but far less often than you would with a liquid polish over a traditional finish.

Note: Any piece of wood you intend to glue, stain, or wax should be clean for the product to properly adhere. If there is the grime of age or any other type of soil, clean the area to be worked on with mineral spirits. (A petroleum-based solvent that won't harm the wood or most finishes and is available in paint stores and building supply centers.)

SCRATCHES. Shallow scratches can usually be hidden by wiping them with a colored furniture polish. The polish is available for light or dark finishes. This is a quick fix and the polish needs to be reapplied fairly often.

To permanently repair scratches, color them with a matching wood stain. The old-fashioned way is to use a toothpick or an artist's brush dipped in stain to color the scratch. Apply one application and let it dry. If the color is too light, apply a second application.

A newer method, and just as effective, is the furniture touch-up pen. Wood stains of a number of colors and shades are available in felt-tip applicators (similar to marking pens). They provide less mess and are easier to use than the canned stain and toothpick.

Whichever method you use, the next step is to immediately wipe off any stain that has spread beyond the scratch. Then let the stain penetrate the scratch and dry.

Next, work paste wax into the scratch. You can wipe a wax-laden cloth across the scratch to fill it, or you can drag the wax across the scratch with the straight edge of a piece of wood or plastic (don't use metal, which might scrape the finish). Let the paste wax dry and buff it. Lightly, apply wax to the entire surface, allow it to dry, and buff it.

DENTS. These are compressed or crushed wood cells. They differ from gouges, which are sections of missing cells. To repair dents, first try to steam them out. This method uses moisture to swell the cells back to their normal shape. First, prick through the finish with a pen in several places within the dent's most depressed areas. This will allow the moisture to penetrate below the finish and be absorbed by the damaged cells. Apply a small amount of water to the dent and cover the area with a damp towel or similar cloth. Press the head of a hot soldering iron, or tip of your household electric iron, to the cloth for a few seconds. Repeat this action if necessary. This will force steam down into the damaged cells, and they should swell back to normal.

We're found that applying moisture and heat to a finish can damage it, requiring refinishing. To avoid the risk of damaging the finish surrounding the dent, we cut out the dent's shape, a little smaller than it actually is, from a sheet of wax paper and fit it over the area. This seals the area beyond the dent from water. Be sure the piece of wax paper is larger than the cloth you use to moisten the dent. (If the damage is too great to repair by steaming, resort to the next method.)

GOUGES. We consider a depression greater than a scratch or dent, regardless of its cause, as a gouge. This includes nail and screw holes, dents that won't respond to steam, burns and other surface blemishes that must be scraped, and any other damaged area that requires filling.

For a burn or similar blemish that has penetrated below the finish into the wood, scrape out the discoloration with a pocket knife blade or utility knife. This will create a depression below the surface line. Don't bother to smooth the scraped area, a rough surface will provide more holding power to the filler. Because the depression isn't great, it can filled with colored wax. You can pick up wax sticks in different wood-finish colors at a hardware store or building supply center, or you can improvise with crayons and save money—the price of a box of crayons is less than one wax stick.

Are crayons as good as wax sticks? Sure, both products are sticks of colored wax. Won't the wood-finish sticks match the furniture better than the standard colors of crayons? Not necessarily. Woods differ, and stains differ, and they are both affected by time. You're not going to get a perfect color match without a little experimenting. If the damage is in a less-than-conspicuous site, you're probably safe with a close match. However, if the area of repair is easily seen, you'll be happier with a better match.

Be sure your box of crayons contains black and white, several shades of brown, tan, yellow, and red. These same crayons can be used to touch up paint nicks on other items.

Needless to say, the surface you are going to fill with warm wax must be upright, or the wax will run off. Oh yes, for a successful fill job you will need to heat and blend the crayons to the right color.

We've read the labels on several color sticks and they say nothing about melting the wax into the depressions. Well, it's been our experience you can't fill depressions beyond a light scratch by rubbing a crayon, or a color stick, into it. This is trying to pack the depression with shredded wax. Simply stated, the results are far from adequate. But don't be scared off—mixing and applying crayons to a hole is (big) child's play.

First off, select the brown or tan crayon that most closely matches the finish you are filling. That color is not likely to be right on the mark, that's to be expected. Slice a little of the crayon into the top of a double boiler. Heat, following the instructions given above under repairing Bone and Ivory. Compare the melted wax with the original color you are matching. It may need a touch of yellow and/or red or a bit of black to darken it. By adding small bits of color at a time and melting the colors together, you'll eventually arrive at the desired shade. When you think you have a good match, take it off the heat and let the wax cool. You will notice the color has changed some—that's the way it will look after it has hardened in the depression. If the shade if off, reheat the wax and add a slice of the color you think is needed. Repeat this process until you've hit the right shade. Remember: you can lighten or darken the mixture by adding white or black without altering the red- or yellow-brown tone you've created. Also, you can always start fresh, having a better idea of what colors to use.

Keep in mind the amount of wax it will take to fill the gouge. It can be very frustrating to have mixed the right colors for a perfect match, only to find you don't have enough wax to fill to the surface.

Apply your finished product by reheating the wax and dribbling it into the recess from a knife blade or spoon. Lightly and carefully, scrape off the excess with a plastic putty knife or, with great care, a table knife. Then gently run your finger over the surface to smooth and blend it into the surrounding area. No sanding is necessary.

If you elect to use a commercial color stick and no color mixing is involved, heat the blade of a putty knife or old table knife, apply the stick against the hot blade over the recess and drip the wax into it. To smooth, follow the steps given above.

If the spot you've repaired is a leg or other surface that's not going to get heavy wear, your work is completed. If the area is on a table top or other place of heavy use, it should be coated with a mixture of one part clear shellac and two parts alcohol. Apply this mixture after the wax has thoroughly hardened. Use a small brush and try not to overlap onto the surrounding area. Give the shellac 24 hours to dry and polish the entire surface with wax paste.

A second method of covering the shellacked patch is to cover it with varnish. The problem with this approach is that you have to varnish the entire surface because there's no way to blend in touched-up varnish.

Our personal choice of covering the wax patch is to spray it with a couple of light coats of clear acrylic. Allow each coat to dry according to the directions on the can. The fast-drying spray we have used advises allowing 5 minutes between coats and one hour to handle. We suggest you allow 4 hours for the acrylic to set firmly before applying the paste wax.

This patching method can be used on any moderate-sized nick, crevice, or hole in a wooden object that has a stained finish.

For painted objects, any color crayon or wax stick can be used for the fill, as you'll be painting over it. After the last acrylic coat has set, lightly rub it with a medium grade steel wool pad so the paint will adhere to it. (Be sure to wipe all of the steel wool dust from the surface before you paint.)

Water-base putty and latex-base wood fillers have greatly improved in recent years, but the older products require more surface area to bond than wax, so they're not appropriate for shallow gouges, small nicks, and the like. So read the label on the filler can for instructions on filling shallow indentations. But for deeper and larger crevices or gouges the older fillers are fine. The putty is in the form of a paste and usually comes in white. Wood filler has more body and usually comes in a tan color. However, both products are available in a few wood shades. You apply either of these fillers to the recessed area with a putty knife. Allow for shrinkage by overfilling unless the directions state there is no shrinkage. When the filler has set, sand it flush to the surrounding surface. To paint or stain, follow the directions on the can—the directions by various manufacturers often differ.

Wood filler is the choice where shaping or modeling is called for or the repair must be made on a vertical surface. It's far stronger than putty or wax and most brands can be freely cut, sawed, and sanded.

Finish Damage

Often, the only problem with a wood piece is a few worn spots that allow the natural color of the wood to show through. Furniture polish with a built-in stain will help hide the flaws for a short time, but they evaporate and must be reapplied frequently. Shoe polish will often cover a spot temporarily.

Our favorite method of covering these faded or worn areas is to touch them up with water colors. It is like blending the crayons (described earlier) but even less complicated, blend the various colors to arrive at a match to the finish color. Use as little water as possible. Dab it on the spot with a small brush and allow it to dry. Carefully wipe off any paint that has spilled over onto the surrounding area with a damp cloth. Water colors turn a slightly lighter shade when dry, but two light coats of acrylic, as described previously, should darken the paint to its wet shade. When all is dry, polish with paste wax.

CIGARETTE BURNS. These blemishes must be scraped away, but take no more of the finish and wood off than is necessary. With a cotton swab, apply a stain that matches the finish of the piece. Fill it in with a thick coat of paste wax. After the filler has dried apply more wax to the entire surface and buff. If the damaged area is deep, follow the directions for gouges.

WHITE RINGS. The treatment for this problem depends on how deep the ring has penetrated. If the mark is shallow, buffing it with a mild abrasive material, such as toothpaste, with a soft cloth should remove it. If this fails, try covering the ring with petroleum jelly and letting it set overnight, then remove the jelly and buff the area with a soft cloth. If the ring is really deep, make a paste of rottenstone powder and linseed oil (both from a hardware store) and rub it into the wood until the spot disappears. Clean the area with mineral spirits and stain the spot if needed. Finish off with paste wax.

Veneers

Thin strips of desirable wood grains, veneers are often glued together in patterns and designs called inlays. Limited use of veneers occurred in ancient Egypt and Rome, but it wasn't until the 16th century that European craftsmen began using them. By the 17th century, veneers were being used to cover whole surfaces, and as finer-tooth saw blades were developed, the use of veneers increased.

Damaged, loose, or missing veneers from inlays can, with few exceptions, be repaired by an amateur—high-priced antique furniture being one of the exceptions. If the piece is loose, remove it. This may require delicately cutting it free with a razor blade. Scrape off all the old glue from the sides and bottom and the surface to which it was glued. Apply liquid hide glue or yellow glue (available at hardware and craft stores) to the under surface and position. Wipe off any surplus glue from the surrounding area. Place an object on the piece to provide the pressure needed for a firm seal. Note: different types of glue may not react (expand and contract) to humidity and other air changes the same way and so may cause more damage. Liquid hide glue and yellow glue were used for joints and veneers until recent years and are the best choice of glue to use on older veneers.

If the inlay piece is damaged, cut out the ruined section and scrape out the old glue from its bed. Fill this area with colored wax, as described earlier, or use filler and paint it to match the original piece. This is not a museum-grade restoration, but if done carefully, it can usually conceal or cloak the repair. If you have access to woodworking supplies, you may be able to match the piece of veneer. Veneers are available in various sizes in an assortment of woods and patterns.

For large sections of veneer, such as table tops, that have lifted at the edges, try to reglue first. Place a damp towel over the area and apply heat with a household iron set at low for 10 seconds. If the spot isn't damp and flexible, repeat the process. When the area gives to the pressure of your hand, cover it with wax paper or plastic wrap and weigh it down with heavy books or other items. Allow to dry for 12 or more hours. If the old glue doesn't take, you'll have to apply fresh glue. You will have to scrape away as much of the old glue from the underside of the veneer piece and the table top surface as possible. Brush on liquid hide glue or yellow glue evenly and press the veneer flat. If the area is larger than the size of your two hands, roll it with a rolling pin or similar device to insure a good distribution of the glue. Next, wipe off any surplus glue with a damp cloth before it dries. Lastly, clamp or weigh down the veneer. Spread wax paper or plastic wrap over the area being glued, and over that place a flat board that also covers the gluing area. If you have clamps, securely clamp the board to the table; if not, pile on a stack of books and let set for at least 12 hours.

Blisters in veneer surfaces can be repaired by making a small slit with a utility knife and injecting glue. If you don't have an injector, pry up one side of the slit and feed in the glue with a toothpick. You can camouflage the mend by making it along a dark line of the grain. With a glue injector (looks like a clumsy hypodermic needle, available at hardwares) insert liquid hide glue or yellow glue. Press down, wipe away excess glue, and weigh down as described in the last paragraph.

Warped Surfaces

Wood that is only finished on one side is subject to warping. The top, finished side resists the moisture in humid air, while the unsealed underside is open to absorbing it. This uneven moisture content in the two sides can cause the board to warp. If the warping is seasonal, wait until the board has flattened and then seal the edges and bottom to prevent further warping. If the warp is permanent, take the board outside and place it, with the concave side facing down, on a wet towel in the sun. Place light weights on top. Rewet the towel and keep the board in the sun until the board is flat. Our advice: don't buy warped furniture.

Sculptured Surfaces

Ornate picture frames and other sculptured pieces can be repaired with plaster of Paris or wood fill. The professional way is to make a mold of the broken or missing section from a good section, and then fill the mold with casting material. This is an involved procedure, so we suggest that you go for the simpler approach of molding the replacement part by hand. This is actually easier than it sounds, and if you ever molded clay or play dough as a kid, you come to the task experienced.

If the damaged area is large, you will be much better off if you divide the repair into manageable parts. The basic approach is the same for a variety of items, so we'll go over the steps we took to replace the damaged filigree on a Victorian frame we picked up at auction and repaired.

The frame measures 30 inches by 36 inches overall, and the antique-gold molding is 3 inches wide. The filigree pattern consists of grapes and leaves done in gesso (plaster of Paris) applied to the wood frame. The frame must have been stored in an attic or basement because it had water damage on one corner and a two-inch damaged spot further down the side.

Our first step was to completely clean away all the loose flakes of gold paint and bits of plaster. Under a dark discoloration we found mold and scraped that off. Next we prepared our plaster of Paris.

We learned years ago from an antiques-dealer friend to use white glue instead of water to mix the plaster. This makes a much superior product that bonds far better. The ideal consistency of the plaster is midway between mayonnaise and peanut butter. The wetter it is the longer it takes to dry, and the dryer it is the sooner it will harden. You want it stiff enough to mold and you also want time to do the molding. Because moisture is absorbed so quickly by the plaster, its best to mix it a little wetter and let it firm-up for a few moments. Be sure its completely mixed—no spots of dry plaster in the batch. Mixing is simple: pour 3 or 4 tablespoons of white glue into a teacup-size container, add an equal amount of plaster, and mix it. You now have an idea of which to add next and also what volume is created. Keep adding the glue and the plaster until you have the right consistency—by that time you will probably have more than enough volume.

While our plaster was setting for a few minutes, we moistened the repair areas with a few drops of water, making them more receptive to the plaster. We gathered together necessary sculpturing tools: teaspoon, paper clip, small water-color brush, ball-point cap, toothpicks, and a damp towel to wipe plaster from the tools.

We spooned in the plaster and began by forming the general shapes of the leaves with the edge of the spoon. The cap off a ball-point pen did just fine with the grapes. As the plaster was hardening, we refined our work with the toothpicks and paper clip (unopened). The dampened brush was used to smooth out the finish. We left it to dry and repeated the process with the damaged corner. There was still more to do.

The following day we improved our handiwork by sanding and scraping the details. The leaves are concave, and needed sanding, and there were burrs on many of the stems, etc., that required smoothing. When that was completed, we applied restoration wax. (A product that comes in several shades of gold, as well as other colors, that you rub or brush on and buff.) The antique gold was a very close match, but not right on. This is a hundred-year-old frame and the gold finish isn't uniform. So we highlighted the whole frame by rubbing the wax across the protruding tips of the filigree, finalizing the job by buffing the entire frame with a shoe brush—with the residue of dark polish.

The frame, with a mirror in it, has hung in our dining room for over 5 years and we love it.

Loose and Broken Appendages

The legs, rails, rungs, spindles, slats, stiles, and supports of furniture (particularly on chairs) can loosen from the pressures of wear, the result of glue drying out, or both. For an example, we'll follow through with the remedy for a chair leg. If the loose leg still fits tightly in place, clean the old glue from the dowel end (the end that fits into the seat) and the socket (the hole that receives the dowel) and apply fresh glue. If the leg fits loosely (wobbles in place), try using a liquid wood sweller, available in most hardware stores. Soaking the dowel in water will swell it, but the moisture will dry up and the piece will shrink again. If you can't swell the leg to fit tightly, move on to shims (wedges).

The preferred shim is one that is inserted into the leg's dowel (the end of the leg that fits into the seat socket) to enlarge it. To do this, you will need a vise, backsaw or hacksaw, drill and bit, and a wood or rubber mallet (a hammer will do if you use a piece of scrap wood to protect the shim as you tap it in). Begin by placing the leg in a vise wrapped with cardboard or heavy material to avoid marring. About three-quarters of the way from the tip of the dowel, drill a perpendicular hole through it with a 1/4- inch bit. Next, starting at the tip of dowel saw—with the blade aligned with the drilled hole, saw down into the hole. The purpose of the drilled hole is to prevent the shim from splitting the leg when it is tapped into it.

Shims can be bought at building supply stores, but they are easily made from scrap wood. The wedge should spread from about 1/8 inch at its bottom to the thickness needed to fit the dowel tightly into the hole. To determine this, measure the diameter of the socket, the diameter of the dowel, and the depth of the saw cut. If the dowel's diameter is 3/16th of an inch smaller than the socket's and the saw cut is 1-inch deep, the wedge should measure about 3/16th of an inch thick, one inch from its lower tip. The shim can be any length, but should exceed the length of the saw cut by an inch or two, and its width should be the same as the dowel—if it's wider it can be cut and sanded to fit after its in place. The length will also require trimming after it has been inserted.

Before you tap the shim in place, slide its tapering edge along the tip of the saw cut until it fits snugly. Measure the diameter of the dowel, and tap again to further expand its diameter to the desired size, if necessary. When the dowel is at the correct size, mark the shim at that point. Now measure the distance between the narrow end of the shim and the mark that indicated the thickness required. If its more than 3/4 inch, trim the excess from the narrow end. This will allow 1/4 inch with which to adjust.

Tap the shim into place and saw off and sand the top and side surplus. Saw, file, or cut three or four, evenly spaced, vertical grooves along the dowel. These grooves should run the length of the socket, but not beyond or they will show when the leg is in place. Their purpose is to provide an escape for air and surplus glue.

Now for the moment of truth. Insert the leg into the socket. If it's too big to force in, trim off just enough for a snug fit. If the fit is still loose, tap the wedge further into the dowel—we've allowed 1/4 inch for this purpose. Once you have the proper fit, spread a thin layer of white glue on the dowel and around the walls of the socket. Tap the dowel back in place and wipe off the excess glue. Allow to dry overnight, and the job is completed.

If the leg or other member that is loose is supported in place by a rail and you can't remove it without dismantling the entire piece, here is a second method to shim. You insert scrap splinters of wood or toothpicks around the loose leg. In order to avoid an eyesore, cut the shims slightly below the surrounding surface with a utility knife. After the shims have been wedged in place and trimmed, apply white glue with an injector.

Yet another way to solve the problem is to drill and insert a dowel (not the tapered end of the leg) through the socket into the loose leg. The best approach is to drill and insert a dowel into the end of the leg; however, the dowel can also come from the side. (The choice should be based on which site is less conspicuous.) The dowel should be cut to a little shorter than the depth of the hole. This will allow room for glue at the bottom of the hole. Apply white glue to both the cavity and dowel, and tap the dowel in place. Use a piece of surplus wood to tap it flush with the surrounding surface without marring it.

Some wobbly joints are caused by worn or splintered screw holes. Rarely will using a larger screw suffice. Actually, the solution can be simpler. Just insert some toothpicks or splinters of wood. If that doesn't solve the problem, fill the hole with wood filler (not putty) and push a guide hole into the center of the filler about the diameter of the tip of the screw and as deep as the screw is long. Let the filler harden and insert the screw. An even better method, but one that requires more work, is to fill the hole with a dowel. Re-drill the hole, drive in the dowel, saw and sand it flush.

Tables and chairs that wobble because their legs are uneven can be leveled by adding a glide (an over-sized tack that you tap into the foot of the leg) to the short leg. These are available at any hardware store.

Hardware

Handles, hinges, knobs, pulls, and other furniture hardware can be cleaned and refinished. Brass and bronze ware can be polished and left as is to develop a patina, or sprayed with lacquer or acrylic to keep the luster. Chromed pieces that have some rust, can be cleaned with steel wool and covered with acrylic to retard the reappearance of the rust. Painted hardware may be steel, iron, or brass. If it's brass, you may choose to clean off all the paint and polish it. Bent hinges, face plates, and the like may be straightened in a vise or by tapping them with a hammer.

Metals

If you haven't had experience in soldering, brazing, or welding, we

suggest you leave repairing broken metal parts that require heat to an expert. However you can replace the parts of broken items, clean off rust and repaint, and patch or reattach non-support parts with epoxy glue. And as mentioned before, you can use epoxy fill to mold missing or broken ornaments.

PAPER GOODS

The end papers of books, and other items with a backing, can be reglued or replaced with little difficulty. If the paper is torn and none of the surface is missing, dab on a little white glue with a small water-color brush and reseat the torn edges so that they overlap correctly. If part of the paper is missing and you have matching paper, place a piece of it over the damaged area, aligning the pattern if there is one, and secure it in place with masking tape. Carefully cut out the patch and the original paper below it with a razor blade or sharp utility knife. Remove the patch and the excess paper, pry out the damaged paper, and apply glue to the spot. The patch should fit precisely.

Torn pictures and posters can best be repaired by first gluing them to a backing. To do this, spray the backing sheet with an aerosol-spray adhesive (available from art supply and stationery stores) and secure the original to it. Roll over the surface with a rolling pin or similar tube for an even bond. Next, pry up the torn edges, align them and press into place. Use the roller again to work out any air bubbles. If there are holes, cut out the patch, as described above, before you attach the backing sheet. After the backing sheet has been applied, fit in the patch. When the glue has dried, you can touch up any discolored areas with water colors or poster paint. To seal in your repairs, spray the entire picture or poster with clear acrylic.

To restore soiled, worn, or faded top edges of books, rub on gold or colored restoration wax. Avoid smearing the wax onto the inside spine by placing masking tape over it, and protect the protruding inside covers, by folding sheets of paper over them. Prevent wax from spilling through to the pages by pressing down on the cover, as you apply the wax. Allow the wax to dry, buff, and fan the pages so they won't stick together.

Creases and wrinkles can be ironed out of paper. However, if the folded or wrinkled edges have become discolored by dirt, you'll see dark lines after the ironing. Going over them with an art eraser should remove them. *Warning: do not attempt to iron out creases or wrinkles on historical documents, first editions, or other valuable paper goods. They should be handled only by restoration professionals.*

Most items will be enhanced by the elimination of folds. We've used this method on less important paper goods that we would not have been able to sell as they were.

To iron wrinkles from paper, you'll need several sheets of construction paper or blotter paper and a spray bottle full of water. Dampen a sheet of construction paper by spraying it with a fine mist of water. Place three or four dry sheets on a flat surface, lay the damaged paper on them, and cover it with the damp construction paper. Iron the damp sheet dry with an electric iron set to permanent press or medium heat. Immediately place a large, heavy, flat object, such as a book, on the sheets until they have cooled off. This will prevent the paper from curling. The ironing can be omitted by placing more dry sheets under the damaged paper and wax paper or plastic wrap over the damp sheet, and laying the heavy object on it. Allow at least 24 hours for it to dry, more if there's high humidity or low temperatures.

Paper mâché objects can be repaired by gluing tears and cracks or replacing sections. To make your own paper mâché, tear newsprint into strips and soak them in water overnight. Drain off all surplus water and mix the paper with flour paste. You can then shape it to the hole you want to fill, or the part you want to replace. However, wet paper mâché shrinks as it dries, so compensate by making the patch or object larger than you need and sanding it to fit after it dries. Drying time is about 48 hours.

Mending tape and hardened glues can usually be removed from paper by heating the underside of the sheet and then pealing or scraping off the tape or glue.

HELPFUL HINTS FOR THE UNHANDY PERSON

☛ Collect several of those brochures, available at hardware stores, that show different wood grains and various stain colors. They'll help you identify woods and stains. However, be aware the colored inks used in printing the brochures are similar but imperfect like-nesses of the actual wood or stain shown.

☞ Keep in mind that wood from different species of trees, different trees of the same species, and wood from different parts of the same tree, usually respond to stains and dyes differently.

☞ When gluing curved or irregular pieces that can't be taped or weighed in place with other methods, try a bean bag. Fill a sock, cloth or plastic bag, with beans. It will conform to convex, concave, or other shapes easily.

☞ You've heard it before, but you should always use paint or other chemicals outdoors or in a well-ventilated space. These products emit fumes that can contribute to respiratory diseases and other health problems.

☞ To prevent damage to screw heads, file the tips of worn screwdriver blades flat.

☞ To prevent hanging pictures and shelves from marring the walls, place self-sticking felt pads on the two inside lower corners. A dozen or so of these small pads come on a sheet or in a packet and are available at hardware stores.

☞ Drawers that stick can be put on a fast track by applying wax or soap, strips of nylon-reinforced packing tape, or embedding thumb tacks, on the drawer glide.

☞ For small touch-up jobs, use an aerosol spray paint, but don't spray it on the object. Spray a bit of the paint into the can's cap, and dab on the paint with a small brush. There's no masking and little mess.

☞ To spray-paint objects without getting paint on your work surface and other objects, construct a spray stall from a cardboard box. Cut off the lid and turn the box on its side. You can also cut off a side, so the top and front are open for better light and visibility. We use the latter and push a cut, unbent wire hanger through the sides from which we can hang small objects.

☞ To prevent furniture from warping, spray or brush clear acrylic or urethane on the unfinished surfaces. This might include the piece's bottom, back, edges, the interior and exterior of drawers, and all hidden structural supports.

☞ Store partially filled paint cans upside down—with the lid hammered tightly closed. This prevents air from entering and drying out the paint.

☞ Dowels and wood plugs that are slightly oversized can be shrunk to size by heating them in a warm oven to remove their moisture. After they are tapped into place and the moisture regained, they will swell back to their normal size.

☞ To sand crevices and other narrow or awkward places, use fingernail emery boards.

☞ The best sanding block—ever—is a blackboard eraser. Cut sandpaper the length of the eraser and wide enough to wrap around it and overlap a bit on top. The palm of your hand will hold the paper in place as you grip the sides and sand.

☞ When your fabric-backed plastic tablecloth becomes worn or stained, don't thrown it away, it will make the perfect drop cloth. It's waterproof, and it wipes clean. If you don't have one, pick one up at a garage sale.

FOUR REPAIR PROJECTS

Transforming the unsightly into something of elegance is usually far easier than the novice imagines. We're not saying that anybody can turn a piece of junk into a treasure. But we are saying you can often refurbish neglected objects into very handsome pieces and increase their value. The biggest problem is thinking the task is complicated and requires esoteric knowledge and a professional hand. In truth, the information in this book and the directions printed on the labels of the various products should provide all the knowledge you need. And yes, experience is good, but careful attention to details is better. And no, you don't need a workshop full of tools, nor a spacious work area, to repair and refinish the various items mentioned in this book.

We aren't craftsmen. We position ourselves somewhere below the handyman class, but we've made repairs and refinished furniture and are pleased with our labors. If we can do it, so can you! Here are four projects we've done, each one different but not difficult .

Maple Table

We picked up a small maple lamp table at a garage sale a few months prior to this writing. The legs are flat—in the shape of slats. Support foot-rails cross between the legs three inches from the floor, and the legs angle in as they rise and attach to the 14-inch square table top, like an A chopped off at the bar. The style is Early American, but the clean, simple lines suggest Arts and Crafts furnishings, to us.

The table was sturdy but splattered with paint, and the top's finish was eaten away in blotches—it would need work. Still, it did have nice lines, so we asked the magic question: "What's your best price?" Without a hesitation, the owner replied, "six dollars." How could we resist?

Our first task was to scrub the table with a liquid dish detergent and water. This revealed a wood tone about two shades lighter and a rainbow of paint splashes that had been hidden by the grime. Nearly all of the paint was on the table's top.

Fortunately, all the paint was latex and we were able get it off with a water-based paint and glue remover. (These products will not remove older oil-based paints, but they work wonders at removing most glues and water-based paints.)

A good wipe down of the entire table with mineral spirits to remove any wax, and we were delighted to see that only the top needed refinishing. To accomplish that, we placed a skirt of newspaper around the legs and on the floor where the work was being done to protect against the stripper.

The stripper we used was a no-wash stripper. This type of stripper doesn't require neutralizing with a water wash-down, which destroys the patina and raises the grain, making it necessary to sand. We applied the stripper to a manageable two-foot area of the top. This prevented the remover from drying out before it could be wiped off. The stripper should be applied with a brush or a rag and allowed to set for a few minutes, then cleaned off. We scraped off as much as we could with a plastic paint scraper. We followed by wiping the surface with paper towels, and finished off by wiping with a soft cloth. *Always wear latex gloves when handling strippers or other harsh chemicals.*

Much of the original stain still showed, but it wasn't uniform, so we applied a matching maple penetrating stain over it. The stain included a sealer to prevent the stain from bleeding through the wood. Following the instructions on the can, we allowed the stain to set for ten or fifteen minutes before wiping off the surplus with a soft rag. After four hours, we applied a second coat of stain, following the same steps. The final finish was an application of paste-wax. We prefer a wax finish because it shows no over-lap marks or brush strokes, and if desired, it can be easily cleaned off and a varnish or other hard finish applied. (A hard finish is a better choice for a surface, such as a dining room table top, that receives spills and heavy wear.)

The table now holds a lamp in one of our studies.

This oak china cabinet was encrusted with grime when it surfaced at a barn auction. When sunshine and bleach didn't do the job, we painted the cabinet and antiqued it.

China Cabinet

About twenty-five years ago, we found a china cabinet at auction for $32.00. It was a Depression piece that suggests Mary and William styling. The cabinet measures 42-inches wide, 48-inches high (plus 13-inch legs), and 15-inches deep. There are three moveable wood shelves. The door is glass, and there are front glass panels on each side of it, and a single glass panel on both sides of the cabinet. The wood surfaces include: the glass panel frames, corner pieces, back, top, and the leg unit.

Much of the finish was crazed (crackled), so we had no choice but to refinish it. The fact that we had just put up new wallpaper in the dining room helped us decide to antique the cabinet in a blue tone that picked up the color of the paper.

We removed the door and the shelves, and sanded all the surfaces smooth. (If we were to do it today, we would use a finish remover/stripper—which is much easier to use than the old paint strippers, available at the time.) Next, we applied a primer coat of paint to the exposed wood, following that with a coat of flat black paint. We did the next step in sections, first painting the top and the three shelves Federal blue. Then, before the paint could set, we lightly streaked the finish with a crinkled-wad of newsprint. We repeated this procedure on the wood, inside and outside of the cabinet. It was necessary to do the blue painting in sections so the paint wouldn't dry before we could antique it with the newspaper.

That was it. We created a beautiful cabinet with an antique finish that has lasted a quarter-of-a-century. Total labor time was about 10 hours, spread over a week. Today, using a modern finish remover/stripper, the time would be about three hours.

Novelty Lamp

A few years ago, we bought a table lamp made of pot metal (scrap metal melted and cast), with a cat as the base, for $4.00. It was charming and only had one fault: a one-and-a-half-inch piece of its tail had broken off. With the wondrous ability of epoxy putty, the repair was both fast and easy.

The epoxy putty that we used came in two bars. One bar contained the resin, and the other the hardener. We sliced off equal amounts from each bar and kneaded them together. Then working it like a piece of clay, we molded the mixture into the shape of the missing end of the tail. We had already cleaned the raw edge of the break on the lamp, so we next joined the pieces. Because the tail wasn't free-standing—all of it rested on the cat's body—it didn't need support while it set. Spray-painting the entire lamp the same color made the mend undetectable.

Humpback Trunk

Several years ago we bought a camel-back trunk at auction. It was made around the turn of the century and probably sold new for five or six dollars. Today, in original like-new condition, this type of trunk often sells for over a thousand dollars. Our trunk, as it now is–completely refurbished–is worth less, but still would bring

The camel-back trunk had seen some hard wear when we bought it. But refinishing turned it into a useful and attractive addition to our home. (The cat was extra—purchased secondhand at an animal shelter.)

a hefty price. Similar trunks, in less than perfect condition, can be picked up at auctions inexpensively. Condition—and how competitive the bidding gets—almost always determine the price.

Camel back, hunch back, and dome are all names applied to trunks with arched lids. Vintage trunks, arched or flat topped, come in various sizes, but the full-size model is about 35-inches long, 20-inches wide, and 20-inches to 24-inches deep (including the lid depth). The interior is commonly papered over a wood shell. Metal and /or leather cover the exterior, which is usually trimmed with wood slats that run perpendicular, suggesting straps. Most of the trunks we have seen have, or had, leather handles mounted on the ends. Locks with ornate face plates are the rule.

Skip any step in the refurbishing procedure described below that is unnecessary. For example, if the interior lining of your trunk is in good condition and you're satisfied with it, ignore that step.

Begin with a general cleaning. Vacuum the inside, wipe out the corners with a damp cloth or sponge. Any mildew should be removed. If the old interior paper is flaked, torn, or otherwise uneven, strip off as much of it as you can. Do whatever is necessary to provide a smooth surface for the new lining. This may require some sanding. If there are gouges, they should be filled in with wood putty. Shallow indentions can be filled by gluing in layers of paper (cut to the desired shape) to the right depth with white glue. Smooth walls are ideal but not always possible. If the interior surfaces still contain blemishes, all is not lost. Heavy material or small patterns will conceal myriad flaws. But we'll get into that subject later. Before refinishing the interior, the exterior should be completed.

Once the inside of your trunk has been cleaned and made ready for a new liner, air it out. Many of these old trunks were stored in basements or attics and have acquired a musty odor. If this is your problem, leave the trunk outside in the sunshine (with the lid open) for several days. This, of course, can be done while you're working on the trunk's exterior. Be sure the inside walls are thoroughly dry before you apply the liner.

Trunks completely covered in leather or imitation leather can be difficult to repair. General deterioration of the material, discoloration, scuffs and tears, and missing panels or sections, are common problems. Replacing the damaged or missing portions with a material of similar thickness and texture and then dying all the panels a darker color is one way to go. A second solution is to glue new leatherette material over the panels. There is a large selection of colors and textures in leather-like materials, and the cost is moderate.

If your trunk is covered with sheet metal, it probably has age marks in the form of nicks, dints and scratches. The scratches should sand out easily enough, but the nicks and dents may require professional skill for their removal. The cost likely will run higher than the trunk's worth.

We have dents in our trunk and we like them. They're character marks, accumulated over a hundred or so years. What stories that trunk would tell if it could talk! Did it begin its service accommodating a young girl's trousseau, or storing the linens of a modest family in a cold-water flat, or as a safe haven for the treasures of an octogenarian's lifetime? We'll never know, but the endless possibilities are always fun to imagine.

Before you clean the outside, determine if any trim or hardware is loose, broken, or needs to be taken off for refinishing. This is the time to remove anything that can't be repaired or refinished in place. Save whatever you take off. You'll be putting it back, or you'll need it to match a replacement. Next, wipe down the surfaces and clean out any crevices. A household cleaner may suffice or you may need a degreasing chemical.

If the exterior finish is rough or spotty, the best approach is to completely strip it off with paint remover. First cover any area, wood trim, or hardware you do not want to strip, with masking tape and paper. Don't use plastic; the chemicals will dissolve it. On the other hand, if the wood trim and/or hardware also needs stripping, don't mask it, strip it at the same time. Work outside or in a well-ventilated room and wear rubber gloves, long sleeves, and old clothes or an apron. Be aware; the chemicals can burn the skin, eyes, and any exposed body area. Because dissolved paint is messy, spread several layers of newspaper over the surface on which you will be working. Follow the manufacturer's directions. Most products can be applied with a brush and, after a few moments, wiped off with paper toweling. For stubborn spots, use a kitchen scrub pad. The process will go a lot easier if you strip one panel or section at a time, wipe it clean, and then move on to the next.

If you elect not to strip but the surfaces are rough with rust and/or uneven paint use sandpaper or emery cloth to smooth down the areas, finishing off with fine (0000) steel wool. If the surface has only minor chips or cracks, work with a medium to fine grade steel wool. Clean rust and paint off hardware such as latch plates, hinges, and corner caps with steel wool. With all abrasives, begin with a grade no courser than necessary, and work down to a very fine grade for the finish.

We did not refinish the wood slats on our trunk. They show some scaring, but we prefer the gently used look. However, if the slats on your trunk are badly discolored or damaged, or you want to paint them, this is the time to refinish them. Fill in holes and wide cracks with wood putty or epoxy filler and sand to a smooth finish. Mask with tape the attached hardware and areas bordering the slats. With a one-and-a-half-inch brush, apply a colored varnish (oak or walnut stain is in the varnish) or a clear acrylic finish, or paint.

With the trunk completely clean and all surfaces smooth, you are ready to begin applying the new exterior finish. Mask off any portion of the trunk not to be painted. If the slats have been refin-

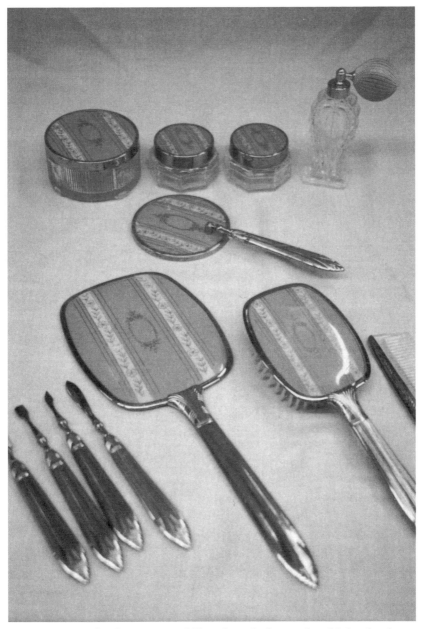

We weren't sure this dresser set could be salvaged when we found it in a box lot. But soap and water, a little glue, and a bit of polishing and the natural beauty came through.

ished, the finish must be completely cured (dry) before masking tape is applied. Any areas that have exposed bare metal, should be covered with a primer first coat. The primer, as well as the finish coat, can either be brushed or sprayed on. We used aerosol spray cans of paint. Our choice of finish was semi-gloss, but you may prefer high gloss or flat.

You needn't repaint with the original dark color. How about fire engine red, or Kelly green, or maybe plum or lavender blue? Your taste and room style set the boundaries.

Remount any hardware that you removed. Pieces to replace those that are broken and need to be replaced can be purchased from a hardware store. If the store doesn't have what you need in stock, they should be able to special order it. Most of the hardware is attached with nails, brads, or pronged fasteners. It's best if these devices do not extend through the inner wall. If they do, bend the protruding point flat with angled hammer blows.

Brass hardware only needs cleaning and buffing. Hardware that was painted or thinly plated can be cleaned and repainted. If you are sticking with the original finish, handles, hinges and latches can be painted the base color; and the ornate locks, latch plates, and strap fasteners painted gold, silver, or bronze.

As far as colors and designs, almost anything goes for the interior. Stripes, plaids, polka-dots, stars, florals, scenes of any type, even solid colors. The material can be cloth; wallpaper; fabric-backed, washable wall covering; or just about any fabric that will conform to the interior surfaces. We used cloth. If the trunk is for a child's room, a washable interior would certainly be a plus.

Measure the interior of the trunk. In order to avoid extra seams, buy material that is wide enough to fit the lid, front and back panels, and bottom. The two ends are narrower and less of a problem, but you need to measure them and the four sides of the lid as well. Remember that a solid color or small pattern requires less material. Large patterns, and particularly a scene, require the extra amount needed to match the pattern. You can economize and simplify the process of installing a scene by using a solid color from the scene on the lid and bottom. If you plan to tuck under the edges for a hem, include the extra inches in your measurements.

Before you cut out panels in the material, measure and fit a paper pattern of the panels in place. This additional time and effort will insure a proper application of the material. In addition, it's the only way to successfully match patterns. If the lid is arched, that panel must be trimmed to accommodate the bulge.

The easiest, and we believe the best, way to attach the new panels is with a spray adhesive. Optional methods are to staple or tack them on. If corners don't fit with precision, use bias tape–plain or ornate. Tack or glue the tape along all the corners and edges.

The final step is to replace the missing or damaged leather handles on the exterior ends. New handles may be obtained at leather supply stores, luggage repair shops, or you can make them from old shoes, belts, or other leather scraps.

CLEANING YOUR TREASURES

Over the years as we've brought home merchandise that was (for lack of a better word) filthy, we've experimented with various cleaning methods. Some worked well. We've had disastrous results with others. As we gained experience with scrubbing and sprucing up our secondhand finds, we settled on the cleaning methods that gave us the most successes. But, we admit, no cleaning method produces a happy outcome all the time.

Throughout this section on removing stains, you'll find the terms, "sponging," "tamping," and "flushing" used frequently in the directions. They're simple procedures:

SPONGING. The simplest way to sponge is to invert a glass pie plate and cover it with four or five layers of paper toweling. Place the stained area over the towels, clean side up. With a piece of cotton dampened with whatever cleaning agent you're using, rub the stain, starting in the center and working to the edges of the spot. Feather the area so that there are no defined rings from the cleaner. During the process, change the paper toweling often so that the staining agent won't go from the item to the paper toweling and then be picked up again by the item being cleaned. If a cleaner is to be left on a spot, keep that spot damp unless the directions say to let it dry.

TAMPING. You'll need a toothbrush for this. Put the stain directly on an inverted glass pie plate (no paper toweling for this one). Tamp whatever cleaning agent you're using into the fabric by using the brush as you would a hammer. This doesn't work well on delicate material, and with any fabric you need to be careful not to be so energetic that you damage, rather than clean, the item.

FLUSHING. Because many of the agents used to remove stains can also cause stains of their own, it's important not to let these cleaners dry on the fabric. To avoid this, you need to flush the cleaners from the stains. If a fabric is washable, you can flush it with water. Hold the stained area under a slow-running cool stream of water. If you prefer, you can rinse the stain in a bowl of water. When you're using the latter method of flushing, change the water frequently.

Removing Stains from Fabrics

Most stains you'll find on secondhand linens will be old stains. Unfortunately, this means they'll be more of a challenge to identify and remove than they'd be if they were fresh. One of the big problems is caused because the article in question was laundered and then ironed with the stain still on it. The extreme heat from an iron will set most stains, making them very difficult to remove. But difficult isn't necessarily impossible. You can achieve some spectacular results if you use the right methods.

Identification—a Little Detective Work

Of course, identification comes first. An old, yellowish-brown stain could be from sugar, honey, mustard, molasses or a like substance. If the stain is sticky to the touch, you can rule out the mustard, which would leave the fabric stiff, but pliable, and dry rather than sticky. This is a good one to eliminate because it's not one of your easily removed stains.

Many stains, such as those that come from most fruits and vegetables, are easy to identify because they retain their original colors or only change slightly over time, while other stains such as blood darken appreciably with age.

Use your nose. It may lead you to the identity of the culprit. Strong odors linger for quite a while. Oil, beer, perfumes, and some cleaners are among the spots that are easiest to identify with a sniff. Your nose can also tell you whether the piece in question has been stored in a damp place for a period of time. The dank aroma probably means the fabric has been weakened and is liable to fall apart when it's washed.

Greasy stains attract dirt, and so they're usually dark—whether they came from motor oil, margarine, or anything in between. Grease soaks into a fabric rather than laying on top of it. There's seldom a crust as there is with most other stains.

What the stained article was used for provides valuable clues to the source of the stain. You're not likely to find a gravy stain on a bath towel or a drape, and it's unusual to encounter a damask table cloth that's been subjected to motor oil or grass stains.

Common Stains

The following is a list of stains that are commonly found on washable items and the steps to take that will, hopefully, eliminate them even if they're old stains. Before you attack a stain, test the fabric in an inconspicuous spot.

ALCOHOLIC BEVERAGES. Sponge the spot with a solution of one gallon of warm water, one teaspoon of clear liquid detergent, and one tablespoon of white vinegar. Soak the item overnight in the solution. Flush the spot in warm water then rinse the entire item. If the spot remains, try sponging it with a mixture made at a ratio of one tablespoon of water to one teaspoon of chlorine bleach. Flush out with warm water.

BLOOD. For an old stain, sponge with ammonia or hydrogen peroxide. Flush well with water and wash the item.

CHOCOLATE. Scrape off any raised residue, then sponge the spot with a solution of one tablespoon of Borax to one cup of tepid water. Rinse well with lukewarm water. If the stain isn't gone, make a paste of Borax and water and work it into the stained fabric. Let it set for an hour or two, then rinse it out with lukewarm water and launder the item.

COFFEE. Without cream a coffee stain usually responds to a solution of detergent, white vinegar, and water. The addition of cream creates a tougher stain. Try sponging the spot with a dry cleaning solvent. (Do this in a well-ventilated area.) After the fabric has dried, launder it in lukewarm water.

EGG. Scrape off the dried particles of egg as well as you can. Then flush the fabric under lukewarm water. If the stain persists, make a paste of pepsin powder (available at most pharmacies). This is a last resort because pepsin can fade or distort colors. Work the paste into the stain and set the article aside for an hour or two. Flush the spot well with lukewarm water and launder the article. Egg white can often be tamped out with salt water, flushing well after and then laundering article.

FRUIT. Avoid soap and water! They'll make the stain permanent. If the spot is light in color, try flushing with cold water. If the stain is dark, sponge it with lemon juice then flush it out with boiling water. If you're lucky the fabric will be strong enough to withstand this type of heat.

GLUE. Soak any stain caused by hardened glue in hot white vinegar for about half an hour. Flush it out with boiling water and then launder the article.

GRAVY. An all-too-common spot on table cloths and napkins. Try sponging the spot with cold water, then sponge it again with tepid water in which you've dissolved a clear detergent. Rinse the spot well with cold water. A really old stain may need to be sponged with a solution of one quart of water, one tablespoon of ammonia, and one teaspoon of salt. Flush the spot well with tepid water before laundering the article.

INK. Many types of ink disappear like magic when they're sponged with a teaspoon of salt dissolved in the juice of a lemon. Flush out the solution, then wash the item. Other ink spots are there to stay.

MAYONNAISE. Sponge the spot with very cool water. If this doesn't do the trick, tamp the spot with cool water. Should the stain still cling, work bicarbonate of soda into the damp fabric. Allow this to set for ten minutes before flushing it out with warm water and washing the item.

MILDEW. Before you try anything else, take the item outside and brush the mildew spots to remove the spores. If you're working with a material that can be bleached, soak the entire article in a solution of one gallon of warm water and one-half cup of chlorine bleach for an hour, then launder the piece with a clear laundry detergent. If the stain is on colored cloth, use a solution of one gallon of cool water, two teaspoons of salt, and one-half cup of lemon juice in which to soak the item before laundering it. (Silk and wool will not take kindly to either of these methods.)

Unfortunately, mildew rots fabric. Any treatment may result in a hole where the mildew has eaten away the material.

MUSTARD. This very stubborn stain resists most attempts to remove it. But if you have a mustard-stained item, you might as well try to rescue it. First, soak the article overnight in a solution of warm water and a clear laundry detergent. Rinse well. If the stain persists, work some glycerin (available at most pharmacies) into the spot. Let the glycerin work for a few hours before flushing it out with tepid water. Then launder the article.

PERFUME. You're most apt to find perfume stains on dresser scarves. To remove these stains, soak a piece of cotton in alcohol. Lay it over the stain. It should draw out the perfume. You may have to make several applications before the spot completely disappears. When this occurs, flush the spot with warm water and launder the entire piece.

RUST. One of the most difficult stains to get rid of, rust spots often respond if you flush them with tepid water before sponging them with fresh lemon juice and finishing by flushing with hot water. If the fabric is strong, try working salt and lemon juice into the spot. Allow it to dry before flushing it out with tepid water.

SCORCHES AND BURNS. When excessive heat from a cigarette or iron leaves a mark, the fabric is almost certain to be damaged, not just stained. But you have a good chance of removing the brown marks by sponging them with a solution of a fourth cup of 3 percent hydrogen peroxide and three or four drops of ammonia. Let this stand until the spot is just damp. Flush it well with tepid water.

TAR. Stubborn, but not necessarily impossible, a tar stain often responds when a lump of solid white shortening is left on the top of it long enough to lift the tar from the item. This usually takes several hours, after which you should launder the article.

WAX. There are several ways you can remove wax from washable items, but first, scrape as much of the substance as possible from the fabric using a dull knife. Then put the stain between two layers of absorbent material, and press it with a warm iron. Move absorbent material frequently so stain is released to clean area and isn't returned to item. If the wax isn't totally gone, sponge the spot with a solution of one-fourth cup of cleaning solvent and one teaspoon of mineral oil, working in a well-ventilated area. Flush this out with straight cleaning fluid. If the spot is stubborn, tamp it with straight ammonia and flush it with warm water. Launder the item in warm water and clear detergent.

Removing Stains From Upholstery

Because upholstery must be cleaned from the front, rather than the back, and because you can't flush the cleaner and the stain out with a liquid, you run the risk of driving the stain deeper into the fabric. When this happens, the offending substance works its way to the surface again and restains the article. The way to prevent this is to work with a small amount of liquid at a time, blotting, blotting, blotting in between applications.

The first step is to analyze the fabric. If it has a nap, treat it gently so you won't crush it permanently. Do you think the material is silk? If so whatever you do is probably going to leave spots. It's even more important to test a small piece of fabric in an unobtrusive area, to make sure that the cleaner won't make matters worse, when you're working with silk.

Unless you're cleaning an upholstered dining room chair, the spot you're dealing with on upholstery isn't likely to be of a food origin. But greasy stains are quite common on living room chairs and sofas—usually on the arms or on the backs. Most of them come from the natural oils that are present in hair and skin, but other stains may be from hand lotion or some other oily substance. Fabric cleaners, available in a supermarket or hardware store, generally will work on these stains. Apply the spotter to the soiled area with a clean rag. Tamp it and blot it with a white rag or paper toweling. You may have to do this several times. When the stain is gone (unless the cleaner's directions state otherwise), sponge the area with a little clear detergent dissolved in cool water. Follow this with several applications of cool water to rinse, blotting well between rinses.

Dry spotters are another possibility. They won't harm most fabrics. These powdery substances, which you can find with other cleaners in most supermarkets and hardware stores, are sprayed on lightly, left to dry, and carefully brushed off. Never apply a dry spotter to a wet stain. You'll get a wet, powdery mess. As with most cleaning solvents, use dry spotters only in a well-ventilated area, and thoroughly air out upholstered pieces before you use them to be certain there's no residual of the toxic fumes. Dry spotters are perfectly safe when used correctly by people who aren't allergic to them.

You may find an upholstered piece that has no spots, but still has that general, all-over, grimy look. The first thing to do with that lackluster sofa or chair is to vacuum it well, removing cushions and getting in all the crevices. Then look for a tag that will tell you whether the fabric must be professionally cleaned (not an expensive deal) or if you can clean it yourself. These tags are usually hidden; because of this, people don't often remove them. Look everywhere, including the underside of the piece. The letters "WS" or "S" on a label mean that you can steam clean the upholstery with a water-extraction cleaning machine. You can rent one of these machines at a supermarket, hardware store, or rental center. If the tag is marked any other way, call in the professionals or go for slipcovers.

If you're cleaning the piece yourself, mix upholstery shampoo according to directions. Do a test in a small, inconspicuous area, allowing it to dry before proceeding. If the test area looks okay, add cleaning concentrate to the solution reservoir of the machine according to the instructions. Working across the piece, apply cleaner by depressing the spray button to release cleaner and slowly moving the head of the machine over the fabric until the entire piece has been covered. *Don't soak material.* Rinse it the same way you soaped, but don't depress the shampoo button. Allow the fabric to dry thoroughly. This will take anywhere from eight to twenty-four hours, depending on the material. If you have a wet vacuum, you can greatly reduce the time by giving the piece a thorough going over with it. This will suck up moisture.

Rescuing a Rug

When you're working on carpets, try not to crush the pile, and before you allow any wet application to dry, brush the carpet pile so that it all goes in the same direction. If you neglect to do this, the area you clean may stand out even though the actual stain is gone.

Many carpet stains are of the sticky variety; the best way to attack them is with a blunt object such as a table knife. Starting at the bottom, rather than the top, of the nap, scrape and lift the unwanted substances up and off the rug fibers. If you start at the top, you're going to push the sticky stuff deeper into the rug, making more work for yourself.

It's unlikely that this scraping is going to solve the problem entirely, but it's a good start. To finish the job, apply a dry spotter, allowing it to stand for about 15 minutes before scraping it off. It's possible that this will take care of the problem. If some of the stain still clings to the fibers (and you're not working with wall-to-wall carpet), put a waterproof material underneath the spot and cover it with an absorbent material, such as layers of paper toweling, and put the rug back over the absorbent material. Working in a well-ventilated area, apply a cleaning solvent. Cover the area with plastic wrap for an hour, then blot well to remove the solvent and the stain.

Although cleaning a rug is similar to cleaning upholstery, you can allow the cleaner to penetrate it because there is no stuffing underneath it. After you've blotted up as much solvent as possible, change the blotting material underneath the spot and rinse and blot until you've removed any trace of solvent (unless the solvent package says it's unnecessary to rinse). Air the carpet well after using any strong chemicals. If you approach rug cleaning too gingerly, you may not penetrate the fibers as deeply as the stain has done. In this case, even though your carpet may look pristine, the stain will work its way to the surface and you'll have to start over.

Cleaning Books

Most books published over the past several decades have been bound in cardboard with a paper or, for a special book or series, a fabric cover on it. But there was a time when most books were bound in leather—at the very least the spines and the corners were done in leather. It is these wonderful, old books that you want to look for on the secondhand market. They're there in quantity, and they look spectacular in a study or living room. Often, however, they are found in dusty, dirty condition. To remedy this, lather up saddle soap and water and apply it to the leather parts of the books. Wipe them dry with a soft rag. It's surprising how easily this makes tired books come to life.

Pictures and Posters

Even framed pictures and posters get dirty over the years. The picture itself may look relatively clean (because the colors and details mask the dirt) and the matting may have an all-over grimy appearance. Or the grime may be visible on the picture itself. In either case, if there isn't a definite stain, try gently rubbing the soiled surface all over with a couple of pieces of soft, white bread rolled up into a ball. As the dirt adheres to the bread, keep changing the surface so that you're not rubbing the picture with a dirty piece of bread, thus resoiling it. This simple procedure should freshen both the picture and the mat.

You'll frequently find finger prints or oily stains on old prints. The first step in eliminating a stain of this type is to rub it lightly

with art gum, blowing the residue from the art gum off the surface
or brushing it off with a clean brush as you work. This should take
care of the stain, but if it doesn't, you can try sponging the stain
with a little lighter fluid. (Do this as a last resort, however, because
the lighter fluid may well make the spot worse. But if the picture
is not valuable and is too stained to display, you have little to lose.)

Many old prints and water colors have brownish-yellow stains
on them. This type of mark is called "foxing" and it usually looks
like it's permanent. However, many foxing marks disappear when
they're treated in the following way: Mix one tablespoon of laundry bleach with two tablespoons of water. With a small brush,
cover the stain with the solution and allow it to work for about ten
minutes. Blot up any excess liquid with paper toweling. Rinse the
brush well and brush clear, cool water onto the affected area,
feathering it slightly beyond the spot. Immediately blot the surface
well. Repeat rinsing and blotting several times to remove all of the
bleach mixture. Place the picture on clean paper towels on a flat
surface. Cover it with more paper toweling and weigh it down
with books or other heavy objects so that the picture lays absolute-
ly flat until it's dry—about 24 hours. If the stain is lighter but still
visible, you can repeat the process. Foxing can be stubborn and
often takes two applications.

CHAPTER SEVEN

A Few Words about Appliances

OF COURSE, appliances aren't usually decorative and many of them such as washers and dryers are ideally kept hidden from view. But appliances of all sorts, large and small, appear frequently on the secondhand market and they are, if not necessities, certainly desirable additions to your home. We've included them in this book because they aren't as easy to purchase secondhand as are other furnishings, and we wanted you to know the pros and cons of recycled appliances and what to look for if you decide to go this route.

Through the years we've learned, mostly from unhappy experiences, that the only two places in which you're apt to find secondhand appliances that have at least some degree of dependability are house auctions and appliance dealers who take them in trade and then recondition them. In the latter case you'll usually get some sort of guarantee or warranty. If one isn't offered, be very wary.

These four modern appliances work fine,
and all of them came from estate sales.

At house auctions, the appliances are almost always operative. Either an estate is being settled and the washer and dryer, refrigerator, dishwasher, and television are in working order and even may be in near-new condition; or the people who are selling the appliances are moving too far away to justifying taking such heavy items; or they are going to a nursing or retirement home where they won't need them. But you won't receive any type of guarantee unless the item in question is still under warranty and that warranty is transferable.

EXPERIENCE IS THE BEST TEACHER

When we were young in the business, we attended an auction in a local firehouse one evening. We'd just purchased a home and were in desperate need of a washer and dryer and a refrigerator. As we entered the firehouse, what to our wondering eyes did appear but a shiny gray washer and dryer set. They looked brand new. "Do they work?" we asked the auctioneer. "I guess so," was his noncommittal reply. We were too intent on getting them to realize he'd promised us nothing.

When the pair came up, we got them for $75. A few items later we purchased an old refrigerator for $10. What buys! But we had no way of getting them home. After convincing another customer, who had a truck, to haul them for us for $10 (which was a great deal more money at that time than it is now), we finally got the refrigerator into our kitchen and our other purchases into our basement. After they were hooked up, we stopped to admire the gray beauties. Then came the acid test of filling the washing machine with clothes and turning on the washer. It filled with water, but nothing else happened. One week and $35 later, an appliance repairman informed us that it wasn't worth fixing. We purchased a new washer. It worked fine, although it didn't match the gray dryer. The inaugural load consisted of nylon underwear. After the washer did its thing, the load was transferred to the dryer. About fifteen minutes later the smell of something burning permeated the house. Opening the dryer revealed an overheated drum. In fact, it was so hot that the underwear had melted and was sticking to it. Apparently one of the heat coils was burned out, which caused the other one to overheat. This is not the way to save money!

The refrigerator, while old, was a gem. It perked along for a couple of years before we replaced it. That was $10 well spent. Still we have never since bought a secondhand appliance anywhere other than an estate auction, a tag sale, or a secondhand appliance store.

PLAYING IT SMART

At one house auction we attended years later, we observed a woman ask for, and get, permission to wash a couple of towels in the washer and dryer that were coming up for sale. By the time those items were on the block, she knew that the appliances worked, and she got them for a good price. Of course, this would have been impossible to do at an auction house.

Before you bid on any major appliance, find out as much about it as you can. Ask one of the auction staff if the age of the appliance is known and if there are any booklets, instructions, or warranties on the item. If you're at an estate auction, these things are probably around somewhere, most people don't throw them out. You may find them in a pile of booklets far removed from the appliance itself.

TELEVISION

Televisions are a standard auction item. At most auction houses, you'll find them plugged in and running. Are they worth the risk? That depends on how much they go for. At one auction, friends of ours got a large console TV for $15. They paid $25 to have it moved to their third-floor apartment. It worked beautifully for six months, then it died. Since they didn't want to pay the price of having a repairman come to their home and tell them it couldn't be fixed, they decided to get rid of it. But it was heavy and they had to hire someone not only to carry it down from the third floor but to dispose of it as well. The object of this story is don't buy a secondhand television that's too large to move yourself. You can take a smaller set home, take it in for repairs, and get rid of it when the time comes. Some older secondhand televisions don't bring in the upper channels. Our main television set is one we purchased new. But we have two other sets, one in the guest room and one in an office. They were both auction buys. We've had them for several years and so far so good. But they don't get much use.

REFRIGERATORS

One of the first things to look for when assessing a recycled refrigerator is dust. If the coils on the back and bottom (which you probably won't be able to see) of a refrigerator are caked with dust the refrigerator hasn't had the tender loving care it should have. A buildup of dust makes a refrigerator work harder and so the motor will wear out sooner. Look the shelves over. Do they show signs of hard wear? Are they all there? Does the refrigerator have the crisper drawers intact? What about the ice cube trays? (If they're the only problem, they're easy to replace.) What about the finish on the refrigerator? Is it all scratched up from abuse or those refrigerator magnets that have become popular? Just because a refrigerator is plugged in and running doesn't mean that it's a good buy. Many refrigerators actually freeze what's in them when they're just about to quit.

VACUUM CLEANERS

Vacuums come in two basic types: the canister and upright. Most people have a strong preference for one or the other. For some reason, both types of these appliance are giveaways at most auctions and garage sales. Check the wheels or runners for breakage. Do the seals seem to fit tightly? Look at the electric cord for worn spots or splicing. If the vacuum has an internal electric cord pulley, test it for easy release and retraction. Plug it in. The motor should sound smooth. Test the power by placing a standard business card on a flat surface and, with the vacuum turned on, lowering the bare nozzle toward a card. At a distance of about one-inch, the card should snap to the nozzle. If the pickup isn't good, check the bag. An overstuffed bag will cut way down on the efficiency of a vacuum cleaner. Inspect the attachments. Are they all there? Do they fit tightly onto the hose? Do they appear to be the original attachments?

SMALL APPLIANCES

Small appliances can be purchased at garage sales, flea markets and auctions. Many people buy the latest gadgets only to find out they don't use them. These can be great buys if you want a hot dog cooker, a sandwich grille (the kind that grills just one sandwich at a time), or a crock pot with a crock that can't be removed from the element for washing (these are the devil to clean!), or any other of the many small appliances that garner favor for brief periods of time. Pressure cookers are another item you're likely to find, but we think the dangers of a used pressure cooker far outweigh any monetary savings.

Toasters, waffle irons, food processors, blenders, microwave ovens, toaster ovens, electric can openers, electric fry pans and griddles, coffee makers, irons—all the small appliances that make modern living a little easier are also plentiful on the secondhand markets. We don't advise buying any of them unless they're at a house or estate auction, an auction house where you know and trust the auctioneer, or a garage sale. And even then, you should always ask if you can plug in the appliance if it's at all feasible. If the seller or auctioneer is reluctant to let you do this, there's probably something wrong with the appliance. Even if it heats up, whirls, or responds positively in the brief period you have to test it, it may not work well when you try to put it to use. Don't go overboard in what you pay for these small helpers. There's no need to; there are plenty out there for reasonable prices. And while no single one of these is terribly expensive new, the savings add up quickly.

Other types of small appliances that you'll find are the examples from other eras. In our opinion, they are more handsome and better constructed than what's offered in the stores today. An old, chrome toaster, for instance, is a much more attractive addition to a kitchen counter than the modern plastic toaster. We've seen some wonderful examples, complete with Bakelite handles, sell for much less than you'd pay for the new models. The only problem is that they only hold two pieces of toast at a time. A short time ago, we were in an antiques mall when a couple came in carrying a loaf of bread. They were looking for a toaster, and there were several nice ones in the mall. After selecting three in which they were interested, they asked if they could try them out. All of them worked, but they liked the even way one of them browned the toast and purchased that toaster.

Waffle irons are another kitchen helper that are fairly plentiful in antiques malls and at auctions. The really old ones from the 1700s are pricey and more for show than use. They were fashioned to be heated over a fireplace. Electric models from early in the 20th century on are more feasible for use in today's kitchens. Although it's not practical to carry a batch of waffle batter with you, you can ask to plug in a waffle iron to see that it heats up. Some of these older electric waffle irons are handsome enough to be displayed on a sideboard in even the fanciest dining room.

Some secondhand appliances seem to have the life span of the average mosquito once they are installed in their new home—others serve well for many years. It's a gamble, and if you're going to buy secondhand appliances, you need to be something of a gambler. But when it pays off (as it often does) the payoff is large.